FROM
CLASSROOM
TO CAREER

FROM CLASSROOM TO CAREER

HOW TO NETWORK, NAIL THE INTERVIEW, AND NAVIGATE FOR SUCCESS

SHIRLEY MORRISON

ALLWORTH PRESS
NEW YORK

Allworth Press books may be purchased in bulk at special discounts for
sales promotion, corporate gifts, fund-raising, or educational purposes.
Special editions can also be created to specifications. For details, contact
the Special Sales Department, Allworth Press, 307 West 36th Street,
11th Floor, New York, NY 10018 or info@skyhorsepublishing.com.

27 26 24 23   5 4 3

Published by Allworth Press, an imprint of Skyhorse Publishing, Inc.
307 West 36th Street, 11th Floor, New York, NY 10018. Allworth
Press® is a registered trademark of Skyhorse Publishing, Inc.®, a
Delaware corporation.

www.allworth.com

Cover design by Mary Ann Smith

Library of Congress Cataloging-in-Publication Data is available on file.

Print ISBN: 978-1-62153-819-6
eBook ISBN: 978-1-62153-820-2

Printed in the United States of America

For Bertrand, my universe.

CONTENTS

FOREWORD

#THERES ALWAYS ANOTHER OPTION

For my twenty-first birthday, my mother surprised me with a trip to Oktoberfest, a month-long celebration in Munich, Germany, where you drink beer in tents and dress up in traditional German outfits of dirndls and leather lederhosen.

The festival originated in the 1800s as a celebration of marriage between a German princess and the king of France. Oktoberfest is now an annual festival that takes over the entire town of Munich for a month. Large tents are put up and the celebration of beer attracts hundreds of thousands of people from around the world. Up to seven million liters of beer gets chugged, some in glasses the shape of boots and some while people dance, linking arms in celebration. The festival is known to be crowded, loud, and international.

In order to get in, you need to wake up at the god-awful hour of 6:00 a.m. to be first in line to enter the tents and start drinking beer. My sister, mother, and I dressed up in our dirndls and proceeded toward the festival area. By 7:30 a.m. the place was already full and people were running around trying to figure out which tents they wanted to enter.

As Americans and first timers at Oktoberfest, we weren't quite sure of the process, but my mother had picked out the biggest tent she could find on the map and said, "Let's go there." So, we walked to the middle of the festival to the biggest tent on the premises with a total of ten thousand seats. It looked like a small village on its own!

As we got closer to the tent, I noticed thousands, literally thousands, of people standing in a line circling around the tent. It was the biggest and longest line I had ever seen in my life. People were pushing up next to each other, impatiently waiting to get their first sip of beer at 8:00 a.m. in the morning.

As we stood at the end of the line, my mother shot me a look I knew too well, letting me know she was not pleased with the situation. My sister and I carefully gave her some space, and made friends with a few college girls in line, discussing our time abroad and patiently waiting our turn until we could enter the tent. We speculated, judging by where we were compared to the entrance, that it would take up to about two hours or so.

All of a sudden, my mother grabbed my arm and said in a stern voice, "Ladies, follow me." She was not only speaking to me and my sister, but also to the three college girls we'd met in line. Being the obedient girls that we were, we immediately followed my mother, no questions asked. Moving quickly, my mother rushed us to the side of the tent and then through a kitchen door propped ajar. None of the kitchen staff seemed to really care as a mom and five college girls passed through. Not only did we skip hanging out for two hours, but we were one of the first groups to pick a table in the tent.

WOW!

We jumped up and down with joy and laughter at my mom's ingenious idea of sneaking through the kitchen door. I don't often drink beer at 8:00 a.m. but I tell you, that morning, that beer was the best ever. Not only did we have the best birthday of my life, but my mother also taught me an invaluable lesson: There is always another option, even if the vast majority of people don't see it.

A friend from university once told me to think of life like entering a nightclub: the majority of people are waiting outside in line with the nothing-I-can-do attitude until finally being let through the main door. Others go through VIP, the rich and privileged, never glancing at people still in the other line. Then you have the courageous and bold who climb through windows or kitchen doors (my mother) with a nothing-stops-me attitude until they are dancing on that main floor. The next day no one talks about the people who stood in line at the nightclub, but everyone knows the legend who found their own way into the club.

It's the same with business and your career. You can choose to be like 90 percent of the population and stay in line waiting your turn. *Or* you can say:

Forget the line. I'll find my own way to achieve my career or the opportunities I want in my life.

My mother used to say, "I don't do lines." I took it literally, like she wouldn't wait in a line at the grocery store or at the Department of Motor Vehicles (DMV). But really, what my mother was telling me was that she'd ensure whatever she wanted, not by waiting, but by taking action. She claimed that "there is always another option" and proved that time and time again. She's one of my heroes.

I'll say this throughout the book: the thing about life that no one quite admits is there are NO RULES. So, taking the kitchen door or climbing through a window may not be the norm to get into Oktoberfest, but it's an option. No one gave us a fine or got mad at us; we just found another way into the tent.

As you read my business book, I ask you to review what I have written with an open mind. Some of the activities may seem different or feel fake or impossible to believe for you now. When I first started my career, I felt useless, like I was not in control of my own destiny. I've learned over these last ten years that regardless of your background, education, tough childhood, or monetary status you are 100 percent in control of your own destiny and, with a strong mentality, you can make anything happen in your life.

I hope that at the end of this book you realize that anything is possible to those who want it badly enough. And there's always an open door for those who believe they can find it.

Life has no limitations, except the ones you make.
—Les Brown[1]

---

1. Les Brown Quotes. BrainyQuote.com, BrainyMedia Inc, 2022.

CHAPTER 1

HOW TO DECIDE YOUR FUTURE

#HOW TO DECIDE YOUR FUTURE

Graduation day was the most surreal day of my life.

On one hand, I was so excited to be leaving university after eighteen years of institutional life. On the other, I was completely in the dark on the journey I was about to begin.

Even though I put on a brave face, I felt terrified of what lay ahead. Here's the short list of things that kept me awake at night:

- Fear of the unknown
- Uncertainty that my knowledge was sufficient
- Doubt of my own self-worth

It was gone, the path so clearly laid out for me: pre-school, elementary school, middle school, high school, and hopefully college. My life was now to be taken in my own hands. No more classes, no more studying, no more research papers, no more grades, and no more all-nighters trying to cram everything into my memory. My biggest worry over the past eighteen years was to get into university, and then once I got into university, to actually pass in order to graduate.

I was now meant to "make the world my oyster," as they said on graduation day.

Yay! I sarcastically thought.

Walking up the stage to get my Bachelor of the Arts (BA) degree, I didn't feel prepared or ready, "sure" that I'd learned enough about the sciences, mathematics, art history, Asian studies, Black studies, chemistry, biology, and Spanish to actually perform in the real world. I felt like, maybe I'd been taken advantage of by the scholastic system—paying four years of university fees to get a certificate (literally a piece of paper), but no confidence that I could stand on my own two feet. For some people, it may have been a relief to leave scholasticism behind, and especially not to pay those ridiculous admin fees, but for me the corporate working world seemed so intimidating.

Another short list of things that kept me awake at night:

1. How to decide on my future
2. How to network
3. How to apply for a job
4. How to nail the interview
5. How to negotiate
6. How to behave once I get the job
7. How to dress for my job
8. How to reach my career/ambitions
9. How to handle relationships and politics in the job
10. How to be resilient
11. How to balance my job with the rest of my life

Was there a class on all of that? Did I miss it in the curriculum? Where was the class that really prepared me for the working world?

Unfortunately for me, there was no class. Instead, it was up to my own judgment and guidance from my mentors on the best way to move forward. At graduation, I had only one answer to all the questions below:

Q: What field do you want to work in?
Q: What job/role do you aspire to do?
Q: What do you want to do for the rest of your life?

A: No idea.
A: No idea.
A: No prize for guessing correctly—no idea.

So, the real question now is: What do I wish I had known then that I know now?

This is where I hope to be of service to you during your transition and wherever you are on your own journey. If I knew then, back when I was a freshly minted graduate, what I know now, it would have helped me with my self-confidence and self-worth. It would have helped me figure out what I wanted out of life and how to go about it. I would go so far as to say it would have helped with my salary negotiations!

Over the last ten years, I've been fortunate enough to meet with brilliant individuals, some at the very top (chief executive officers, chief information officers, chief technology officers, etc.) and others in the start of their career, climbing the corporate ladder. The one thing that stays consistent with all these individuals is that their career does not just go one way; it's up, down, a few steps back, one to the side, then ten steps forward. Rinse and repeat.

It's a journey that becomes a pilgrimage in a way. There is no endgame in your career; having goals and setting key performance indicators is a great way to see your progress, but sometimes you find yourself in a completely different place compared to where you set out from or you find that your desires have changed. You need to come to terms with the fact that, like anything in life, you will have great moments in your career and exceptionally low times. I've only been at this career thing for a little while, and let me tell you it's been a roller coaster, mostly uphill, but some steep drops that were unforeseen.

As General George S. Patton put it, "Success is measured by how high you bounce when you hit bottom."

You could even go as far as to compare your career to traveling around in a foreign country. At first, everything is unknown: what to do, what to say, and how to behave culturally. Generally you learn it all the hard way: you're in the wrong part of town and it gets hairy, you misunderstand the start time for the expensive tour you booked and miss it, or you get taken to the cleaners so often that it just starts to get boring. Then after a few months you start to get the hang of traveling, what to do, what to say, and how to behave. If you stay for years, you become the expert other travelers look to for advice.

With a new job or role, everything is foreign at first until it all starts to make more sense. If you stay long enough in that role, you may become the most knowledgeable person. It might seem hard to imagine now, but life has a way of allowing you to reach goals without you quite realizing it, as it usually takes place over many years and only after many obstacles are overcome.

There are a few misconceptions that I want to nail on the head before we go any further. My goal is to coach you on the rules and etiquettes that help propel your career in the right direction. So you won't feel like I did, like you're flailing around, struggling and unsure of your profession and/or next professional move. Most importantly, this guide is to give you the resources to make your field of choice and employment a success today.

Misconceptions

First off, we need to cover the biggest misconception in the world. For most of my life, it was my understanding that adults had it all figured out: they knew who they were, what they wanted from life, how to behave appropriately in every situation, how to be a parental role model, and how to have a job. No adult ever admitted to me over the years or even insinuated the reality that NO ONE HAS ANY IDEA WHAT THEY ARE DOING. All adults are making it up as they go along. Slowly, over time, learning and growing, they become the competent human beings we see in our society. So if they say they know exactly what they're doing, then they are either a) delusional or b) lying.

Now, here's the research behind this blunt statement: The truth is most of us, deep down, feel as if we are just winging it. One great example is from the remarkable Maya Angelou, who stared this insight: "I have written eleven books, but each time, I think 'Uh-oh. They're going to find out now. I've run a game on everybody and they're going to find me out.'"[2] Although Angelou was very

---

2. GoodReads. Maya Angelou > Quotes > Quotable Quote. Good Reads. June, 2022.

talented and highly regarded, she was also courageous in admitting her own self-doubts and the fact that she didn't always feel remarkable. Maya Angelou, like many of us, was making it up as she went along.

In life, we are all encouraged to face our fears and swim into the depths of the unknown. The trick to success is eliminating the nervous feeling that you are in over your head, maybe even drowning. The comfort is that everyone, no matter who they are, is feeling it too.

Let's take the stereotypical couple. They meet, fall madly in love, and then one gets pregnant. They'll have little to no experience with newborn babies. Now, let's say you are their firstborn, so they have no experience with kids. If we stick to the stereotype, maybe they babysat, had siblings or cousins, or had been around their friends' kids before, but they might not have spent hours alone with a child. They had no previous experience raising a child, and no knowledge of how to discipline or properly correct a child. Do you think they knew how to raise a baby? Or how to handle toddler tantrums? What to do when their kid is sick? What to do when their teenager (a.k.a. you) decides to run away for the weekend? The basic general answer to all of these questions is your parents completely made it up as they went along. Since your birth, your parents have been creating rules, showing you standards, teaching you morals, and insinuating that they know best—when really, they were completely and wholeheartedly fabricating parenthood.

Another great example is the president of the United States of America. Do you think when Barack Obama or Donald Trump were voted into the Oval Office they had any idea what they had to do? Sure, they had led a campaign about "Making America Great Again" and put hope into the American people for "change that we can believe in." But did they really know how to make these things happen? Did they fully understand their role and how to play it? Or did they too make it up as they went along? Changing ideas and legislation and working with other governments for a better outcome, a better world. Do you think that it's possible that the presidents had it all under control, when really, they too were learning as they grew into their role?

The last example I will use is your boss (or future boss). Now, unfortunately for all of us, we usually don't get to choose our boss. Sometimes you get lucky and get a good one, and sometimes you don't. Bosses tend to be people who have done the job that you're now employed to do; they tend to have experience and have therefore been put in a management role. Do you think once your boss started in a management role, they knew what they were doing? How to manage people properly? How to teach and mentor? Or are they too pretending, learning, and becoming, just like your parents and just like the presidents of the United States?

The fact that no one has any idea what they are doing should give you comfort. It makes your parents, the president, and even your (future) boss seem more human. At the end of the day, we are all just people trying to do our best, in whichever role we find ourselves. It's important to keep a perspective on the roles that you play in your life and remember that growing into a role is a natural occurrence for everyone.

Now, it's your turn to go *From Classroom to Career* and your desired future self.

"Nothing is IMPOSSIBLE, the word itself says 'I'M POSSIBLE!'" How to envision your future:

The crazy part about starting to look for a job is that, before you get it, you need to be able to envision yourself at the job. This is extremely difficult, especially if you are like I was and have never really had an office job before. Picturing yourself doing the day-to-day of this role, whatever it may be, allows you to start to envision your future. The best analogy I can come up with is when you picked where you wanted to go to college. Before you went, you had a vision. You imagined yourself on campus, in class, and living in dorms with other like-minded students. Yet, as a soon-to-be high school grad, you may have had no idea how to make this college vision a reality; you just started, taking one day at a time, putting one step in front of the other, learning and correcting until you've reach your vision and your goal. Usually they are different and even better than you ever could have imagined.

So, get excited, because who knows where this journey will take you!

Stop worrying about the question your parents, friends, next-door neighbor, and the person at the coffee shop keep asking you: What are you going to do after graduation? Geez; if only I'd had some cash for every time some nice person asked me that! Instead, the only thing I got was anxiety every time this question was asked. A good friend of mine, Matt, handled the question with a response that immediately stopped the conversation from going any further.

Question from stranger: What are you going to do after graduation?

One-word answer from twenty-two-year-old Matt: Retire.

A.k.a. none of your business. As a society, we need to encourage each other to stop putting pressure on ourselves and focus on being happy. Focus on the big picture of life, not just one aspect.

The real question from people should be: "What will your future self be?" Our society is so focused on the next step that people forget to look at the big picture. It's time to step back and envision your future. This is where all the magic starts and when you realize the power of visualization in your life.

I want you to forget about what your teacher, friends, mom and dad told you, what they thought YOU should do in your life, or even what you think you "should do." Instead, let's focus on you and your personal desires and wants from life—no outside opinions or pressures. Just you and your "wants" from life.

> *Imagination is more important than knowledge.*
> —Albert Einstein (1879–1955), German theoretical physicist

Here's a great activity for you to do. It's fun, and it'll help you envision your future:

- You'll need your computer or tablet.
- This exercise should take anywhere from thirty minutes to an hour to complete sufficiently. Please make sure you have sufficient time to complete this activity in its entirety.
- Grab your computer and/or tablet and go to: www .canva.com.
- Please note: You do not need to sign up for a membership on www.canva.com.
- Click on "make a poster."
- Title the poster: My Vision Board.
- Let's start visualizing your life with pictures. Feel free to add words or sentences that mean something to you as well throughout this activity.

- It is very easy to search on Google for images, save them on your computer, and then paste them directly onto your storyboard, as well.

Before we begin this exciting activity that will help guide us to what you really desire from life, I want you to sit back and take a deep breath. Make sure you are in the right state of mind for this activity and that you have time on your hands to complete the storyboard.

In your mind, start to compartmentalize your future life. What will be in your life? What will the compartments look like? For this mind-provoking activity, think GIANT, think big, think ambitiously, and even dream a little. Put yourself out there and try to picture your desired future self. What would that look like for you? You can always change your mind or decide that you don't want/ desire something different down the line. This activity is supposed to be thought-provoking, fun, and exciting. Reach deep inside and listen to what your heart tells you it wants.

This is not just about your job. Our society is so focused on people's occupation we sometimes forget to think about our overall happiness at home, with friends, love life, money, health, etc. Life is complicated and in order to be happy and successful, you need to look at the big picture and not just one segment.

Some questions below to get you thinking about your future self:

Relationships (partners, family, friends)—Who will be your close connections (family, friends, kids, and/or a partner)? Will you have a partner? Be married? What would this person look like? What type of person will they be?

(If you currently already have a partner, think about taking your relationship to the next level. What would that look like? Engagement? Wedding? Kids? Dogs? Buying property together?) Will you be close with your immediate family or close with your partner's family? Will you have a large group of friends all over the world or a small group of quality friends?

Location/cultural environment—Where in the world will you be living? What culture will you participate in? What language or languages will you speak? Specific country? City? International lifestyle? Or do you prefer the countryside? How will you live? Will you be living in a small cottage or a large mansion? Maybe you prefer to be close to the beach? Or in the mountains surrounded by the snow?

Health—How will you look physically? How will you feel physically? How will you feel mentally? Fitness goals? Become a gym rat? Run a marathon? What would you need in order to be mentally stable? Work with a therapist? Many people take health for granted. However, those who have been sick understand the importance of good health, physically and mentally. If you are sick, what would healthy look like for you? How would you feel? What would you be doing? How would you be different from your current state? Do you want big muscles? Maybe you want to lose weight? How do you picture your future self?

Purpose (volunteering)—What speaks to your heart? How will you be of service to the world? Volunteer? Write a book? Or give a speech to thousands and inspire? Or maybe it's to raise your children to be good citizens of the world? Run for public office? Work with underprivileged children? Become a parent through adopting a child? What do you stand for? Is there something that speaks strongly to your heart and/or something you want to change in the world?

Everyone has a purpose, something that they live for and gives them a sense of pride and accomplishment. Try to start to uncover what your purpose may be. Again, it may change or evolve into something else as you go on your journey, but try to understand what it may look like for you at the current moment.

Monetary fortunes—How much money do you want to make? How much money do you want to save? What do you wish to buy with your monetary fortunes? A house? Stocks? Maybe a few watches? A flashy sports car? If you are in debt, how long until you become debt-free? Make enough to pay rent and live with your best friends? Do your interests align with the average current salary and your expectations? Maybe money is not important to you and you prefer to live a simple life, by doing something that pays less, but is meaningful? What are your values with money? Is money important to you or not in your life?

Money is a tricky one for this activity. Basically you need to sit down and work out your finances before you decide really how much you need to make. Calculations need to be considered, like how much do you eat out a day/ week/month? Do you spend money on coffee each day? Do you go on holidays? Once you have a better understanding of your outgoing costs each month, you can then start to work out a salary to fit the lifestyle you wish to have in the future. Initially, your salary will be the lowest of your life (typically) as you're just starting out. Make note of this, but start to imagine what you will be spending your new income on once you land that dream job. Throw out a figure on your storyboard that feels like a reach. Remember we are thinking GIANT here.

Employment—If you could picture your future job, what would you be doing? Would you be working outside or in an office in front of a computer? Would you be presenting to the room or at the table listening? Would you be creating ideas with words or drawing them? Working with kids or animals? Helping people or asking for a sale? Would you be required to go back to school in order to get your future dream job? If yes, what would you need to do to get into the right school, such as (for Americans) GMAT test scores—what score do you need? Are you planning to be a lawyer or doctor? What would you need to do to get into your desired profession?

Now that we have had a run-through on some compartmentalizations of your future self, let's search through the Internet and pick out pictures or images that speak to your future self. I want you to get creative here. Any image or picture that speaks to you and what you desire in your future, save it on your computer and then paste it onto your Vision Board.

- Find a picture or photo that relates to your desire.
- If you are unable to find any picture on www. canva.com, then go off the site. Open another web browser. Go to www.google.com, click images, and start looking for the exact image of what you want in your life.
- Once you find the image, copy it onto your clipboard or save it onto your desktop.

- Go back to your vision board on Canva and upload or paste in your image.

Look through the pictures/images online and start with one life compartment and complete it before you move on to the next. Take your time, looking through the pictures on the Internet, and start to envision what your future will look like. Who and what will you become? Try to get pictures or images that are as accurate as possible.

Here are a few examples to get your creativity flowing:

Example #1 desire: Your future self wants to buy a house out in the countryside with a porch near your parent's home in the Cotswolds, Great Britain.

Example of pictures: There is picture of a house for sale in the Cotswolds that is your dream house. It doesn't have a porch, but you can search Google for a porch and paste it next to the house. Additionally, write the name of the exact town where you want to buy your house in the Cotswolds or you could even paste a map and make a star where your house will be. Put the house, name of the town, and porch together on your board.

The key is to try and be as detailed and exact as possible. There's no need to be perfect, but add as much detail as you can and/or want.

Example #2 desire: Your future self is completely debt-free, has a savings of over $50,000 in the bank, and is on vacation with a glass of wine in hand.

Example of pictures: Find a man/woman on vacation, looking happy and content with not a worry in the world on his/her face. Make sure it's a vacation you would want to take (maybe it's hiking, on a beach, or in the snow).

Write debt-free and stick that to or around the man/ woman on vacation. Make sure to say DEBT FREE and NOT "No more debt." We want to keep everything in a positive language and attitude. Put the amount you want to save, $50,000, near the images or maybe find a check online and write the amount of money you will have in your savings account. Paste all of these pictures together as another compartment. Note: Write or place the check with exact dollar amount you want to receive.

Example #3 desire: Your future self is the CEO of an international law firm specializing in relocation for foreign people.

Example of pictures: Find a student or maybe a graduation cap to visualize yourself going to law school. Try and specify which law school you want to attend and place the name or the location in your visualization. Maybe search for a stack of books, which represents all the studying you have ahead. Get a photo of a foreign student (whatever that looks like to you) and place a road between them to their location. Feel free to use a photo of yourself, as if to envision yourself helping the student with the relocation. Now, to be the CEO, maybe you can find walking steps that shows your progression in the organization. Maybe you write Legal Director, then Head of Legal to CEO on the steps.

Again, get creative here. This is your storyboard and it really only needs to make sense to you. Be as creative and specific as you can so that when you look at your storyboard you continue to remind yourself of your future desires.

Example #4 desire: Your future self is married to a tall, handsome, and kind man. You have four children together.

Example of pictures: Find a man in the magazine that is your type physically, or a photo of something he is doing in the picture that you also enjoy doing and that you would hope you would do together (ex: bike riding, going to concerts, going out with friends). Include in the photo a picture of a happy family with four kids. Also find an engagement ring and add it to the collage.

Example #5 desire: Your future self wants to run a marathon.

Example of pictures: A medal, which would represent your completion of the marathon. Find a picture of a man or woman running on the road as if in training. Place the time you want to hit when you run the marathon (example: under five hours) under the picture.

Example #6 desire: Your future self wants to heli-ski in the alps in Japan.

Example of pictures: Mountains with snow on them. Find a Japanese flag and use a picture of yourself skiing. Find a picture of a helicopter and put the collage all together. Maybe put a picture of Japanese sushi in the collage as well to represent all the yummy food you will eat there.

Add as much detail as you can to help the magic of visualizing your desire and turning it into your reality.

Putting the Compartments Together

You should have a few different compartments (at least five or more) that are spread out on your vision board. Make sure that each specific compartment is a collage on its own. For example, for the partner compartment, the ring, the handsome man, and happy family are all pasted near each other. Take a look at the example on the next page.

My Vision Board

This is an example of my storyboard from two years ago. As you can see, I had: Buy a property in London (CHECK), meet my fiancé (CHECK), publish my book and sell one million copies (in-progress), and receive a check for one million dollars (in-progress). I fully believe I will do all of these things on my storyboard, especially since

I've been looking at it for the last two years! Half of the things I wanted have already happened (two/four)! Keep in mind, the timing of many of these desires all depends on how much you want it and the positive energy you put toward it.

Make sure to: Arrange the pictures together and put in as much detail as possible. For example, for meeting your partner and falling in love, your storyboard could look something like this:

You have a woman and man holding hands in their wedding outfits, symbolizing the marriage. The man is tall and handsome with a beard, someone you would find attractive. There is also a picture of an engagement ring with the word "love" below. It's very similar to the ring you may desire.

For a compartment on buying a house, it can look something like the following:

You can paste a map and pinpoint the exact location of where you want your property to be located along with a suggested house that you would want to buy. Feel free to even add in some furniture pictures, giving examples of what you will fill the house with once you have the property.

For how much money you want to make and save in the bank, write yourself a check:

Make it something that's a reach for you, but that you can picture coming into your bank account in the future.

For your career ambitions, think about what you want to do and what you want to happen. Here's another example:

1 MILLION COPIES SOLD

Write a book, sell one million copies, help fight the gender gap by being a big earner, and one day make it onto a famous daytime talk show. You can have the piles of your book for sale with a sentence below stating how many copies will be sold. A little glass of champagne represents your ambition and goal to celebrate once you reach a million copies sold and complete your interview on the talk show.

As you saw, make sure you are keeping each compartment together and then place them around each other.

The reality about vision boards is that you can ask for a specific timeline—for example, get the job, then buy the house, then marry your partner, and then have children. The reality, however, is you may get all these things but not in quite the order you wanted. Perhaps you get pregnant first, then get the job, then marry your partner, and then buy the house of your dreams. The biggest thing is putting what you want out to the world and ASKING for what you desire in your life. Try not to focus on the timing of your desires, and instead focus on what's most important: the how. The world will hear you and respond to your desire.

Why Does a Storyboard/Vison Board Work?

The purpose is to now have a visualization—a picture of what you want in your life. Once you have a picture, you can now work toward the outcome.

> Thoughts create emotions.
> Emotions create actions.
> Actions create outcomes.

You have thoughts about your future, which you clearly just demonstrated from putting together your storyboard. When you put down the pictures and started imaging yourself having these things—did you feel good? Did it make you feel happy or excited for your future? What emotion do you feel when you look at your storyboard?

Happiness? Excitement? Butterflies?

By putting emotions behind your thoughts, you start to create an action—whether that's going back to school or to start training for that marathon. The outcome might not happen immediately, but the actions help you to take steps toward your goals.

Thoughts are power. The power behind thoughts needs to be talked about more in our society. Thoughts are one

of the most powerful and important attributes to your success. How you think and how you feel (emotion) directly
correlates to the outcome of a situation.

He can who thinks he can, and he can't who thinks he
can't. This is an inexorable, indisputable law.
—Pablo Picasso (1881–1973), Spanish painter and
sculptor

CHAPTER 2

HOW TO NETWORK

#HOW TO NETWORK

It's not who you know; it's who knows you.
—Anonymous

Let's start with the elephant in the room: the COVID-19 pandemic has changed the world. In 2021, over 67 percent of professionals believed the pandemic would change the way we work going forward. The old ways of networking through a handshake and swapping business cards have now morphed into Zoom calls and digital signatures with your information.

How do you network in a virtual world? What is the correct etiquette? Being in a virtual world can be awkward and unnatural. Unfortunately for many of us this is our reality now, whether we like it or not. There are some people who love working in a virtual world and are finding a better life balance by working from home. The world has realized that even in a lockdown when we can't meet face-to-face, we can still interact. We can still do our jobs. We can still get promotions. Close deals. Find another job without even meeting with the hiring manager in person. I mean, that alone is outstanding.

We are not going to go backward; most companies are now looking at a hybrid approach where people may (or may not) come into the office for two or three days and, the rest of the time, they will continue to work from home. People from all over the world are moving out of large cities and will now have the chance to live wherever they want and still have good jobs. Jobs that allow them to work from anywhere.

What is different about a virtual world? Well, for one thing it's more preparation than being natural and in-person. You have to think in advance of your background, the lighting, where you are, and how you look on camera. The whole feeling of the room and/or using your social skills in person are gone. Being able to touch or lean into the conversation and use your body gestures sometimes do not translate in a virtual world. Where to look on camera? How to stare into the screen in the correct way? I've made a little key below to help you as you start to network in a virtual world.

Virtual Meeting Tips and Rules for Networking:

- Spend the first five minutes getting to know each other—talk weather, sports, acquaintances, etc.
- Use the platform of choice from the person you are trying to network with (Ex: Skype, Microsoft Teams, Google Hangout, Zoom, etc.).
- Check audio settings/download the platform before the meeting.
- Have dial-in options available.
- Do not use backlighting.
- Use a non-busy professional background (a.k.a. don't be in your room with an unmade bed).

- Manage the time appropriately; never go over unless you ask for permission. Be conscious and considerate of the person's time.
- Take notes with the plan to follow up.
- Get on the platform fifteen minutes before your meeting.
- Wear bright colors; think red or light blue, which will help you stand out and be memorable on the call.
- End the session on time or earlier if possible.
- Have your camera ON (ask in advance if it's OK to have the camera on).

Networking is an art form whether you are doing it virtually or in person. It's something that forms and changes as you grow as a professional; your network is entirely in your hands. Humans are social beings, and human connection is more valuable than any university degree.

Networking in a professional setting, whether that's virtually or in-person, is very different than socializing with friends and family. When you are networking professionally for a job, you need to prepare for the conversations you are about to have, even for informal chats. This means that you have clarity and can, at the right moment, present yourself in a relaxed manner. Know the answers to the next list of questions. Memorize them. Practice them. Be that boy/girl scout and be prepared.

- Why are you networking? What are you looking for in a potential job?
- What type of people are you looking to network with? And why?
- Who are the key people you want to get to know?

- What do you want to achieve professionally?
- What is your ultimate goal?

These questions are valid and can help you start to paint a picture of your potential network.

A few things can help you get an idea: look up the type of people you want to connect with on LinkedIn, read about the company or organization they are working for, make a list of genuine questions you would like to ask, and things you would like to learn about if you were to meet with this individual. Then review this person's profile on any social network, scanning through the information. If you ever meet this person, you'll be prepared with a little insight about them that they didn't have to tell you. It shows that you did your homework, proving that you care and are interested to learn more.

Do you have a LinkedIn (www.LinkedIn.com)? If not, it's time to create a profile. Put down your degree and any interests on the page. You want to start to build your online résumé. Make sure to put an up-to-date professional photo on your profile, so people can have a visual of you and remember you. As the saying goes, "a picture says a thousand words." There should be two photos on your page, one a headshot, which is the main photo, and the second is your background photo. Now, this can be a picture of your city or college, or something that means something to you and grabs people's attention. You want to start to build your professional presence online, even if you feel you don't have a lot to put on the page initially.

Take time to write a little summary about yourself and your interests on LinkedIn. The summary should be a chance to tell your story, your passions, and your expertise. Start to connect with friends and family members on the site. Lastly, spread endorsements and add your own. This can build confidence for you and your online presence as you start to look for a job. Feel free to check out my own LinkedIn at: https://www.linkedin.com/in/shirleymorrison/ and feel free to use any of the wording when you make your own!

Some people find that networking makes them feel like job seekers, that is, as if they have a need or are in a weak position. Networking then feels like a public declaration of this need and weakness, and the networker then thinks that they come out looking bad. But this is not true. If you feel like this, it needs to be squashed here and now! People are continually looking for good people to hire and train. Some even prefer to hire recent graduates and give them firsthand training to suit their company needs and requirements. To be clear, every person in the world goes through looking for a first job, feeling uncomfortable, having to network in some capacity, and asking others for advice/help. So stop making excuses and start to become a networking guru!

At the start of my own networking journey, it felt bizarre—almost odd—and forced. Nine months before my graduation, my parents called me. They told me it was time to start looking for a real job. I was like, "I've nine more months still!" They laughed and told me it takes about nine months to get a job. I thought, *That's ridiculous. It can't actually take that long to find a job.*

Their suggestion was to make a list of my dream jobs after college and send it to them. It was a concise list:

1. Teach English—I had studied abroad in Spain and had become really good at Spanish. Maybe I could

move back and teach English? Likely it wouldn't pay well, but could it be fun?

2. Sales—I really liked people and working with others. Maybe I was a natural salesperson?

3. Be a doctor and help others—might need more classes for this, as I did only take Biology and Chemistry 101 and had refrained from taking physics, and the rest of the required courses for a Biology degree. Maybe I could look at med school? Not a big fan of another eight years, though.

The unmistakable standpoint was . . . "Shirley, go for number two."

So nine months out, I started to look for a sales job with a start date of June 15 for the following year. Now one thing I did not realize at the time was that looking for a job when you really don't need one (yet) eases tension all around. People want to talk to you because you're not asking them for a job right away. You don't need anything but merely want information and help. When you need a job, energy runs high and the pressure is on. Looking for a job nine months before you actually need one makes the process easier and comfortable for all parties involved. Needing something can sometimes send out the wrong vibe and energy—you can seem desperate and push people away.

My parents suggested I give three of their acquaintances a call. I decided to look for a sales role in three different industries that were of interest to me:

- Financial Services = Chance to make some money
- Technology = Interesting field, while also a chance to make some money

- Renewable Energy = Saving the world, trendy industry, while also a chance to make some money

At the time, back in 2011, there was a significant movement toward renewable energy. PG&E (a large utility company in California) was hit with legislation that 2 percent of their energy was required to be sustainable energy. I had no degree in renewable energy; I was an International Studies major, which really held no relevancy.

It is good to note here that over 50 percent of people who graduate from college never actually use their bachelor's degree. So don't sit there and say, "I can't get that job because I didn't major in it." Most people never use their major and get jobs in fields they had no prior knowledge of or experience in.

My parents had a friend whose son started a business in renewable energy. They told me to call the son and talk with him. I was hesitant and stated, "I don't even know him. I feel weird calling him out of the blue."

And the response from my dad was, "People love to help other people." My thought immediately was, *What does that even mean? This guy doesn't know me; he'll probably think I'm weird for even calling him and wasting his time.*

Then I started to really think about this statement: People like to help other people. The day before, I had helped my roommate prep for her date. She'd been nervous, and we'd talked through scenarios of what to say on the date. It might sound silly, but I felt honored that she had come to me for help as we lived in a house of seven women, but she had chosen to go to me for advice. Another memory of how I helped move my little brother into the dorms, and then he asked for the low-down of what was cool and not cool to do in university, stayed with me. In both instances, I felt a sense of pride in coaching people who had asked for my guidance. It didn't feel like a burden when they asked for help; quite the opposite. I would even go so far as to say that not only did I like it, but I loved it.

It feels good to know that we helped someone else, that we played some part (even if it's minor) in their happiness in life. People feel a sense of pride when you come to them for coaching and guidance. Think of your own life. Has someone ever come up to you and asked you for help in their personal life? How did that make you feel? Did you turn them away? Or did you take their situation seriously and gave them as much consultation as you could?

Back to my story—my dad helped me prepare for the call. I would talk about how I loved the renewable industry (which was right—I took a course on it in college). I would potentially like a job in the industry once I graduated in nine months (also correct), and wanted to start talking to people in the industry (which I was trying to do). And lastly, did he know of any renewable companies that were looking to hire good people?

Finally, I dialed his number. To my surprise, the call lasted a firm twenty minutes, and his responses surprised me. He was more than happy to talk about the renewable industry, which was quite obviously his passion. He also told me that his company was not hiring at the moment, but two companies in the renewables sector that he thought highly of were.

He point-blank gave me the general managers' names at both companies and their cell phone numbers.

Like, WOW!

The words, "people love to help other people" played in my head. I immediately looked up both of the contacts on LinkedIn and prepared myself. I would call my new connections and ask if I could meet with them in San Francisco.

Now to be brutally honest, at the ripe age of twenty-two years old, I didn't feel at all confident in talking to businesspeople. I mean, I was still in college. I'd barely passed my Art History class, dropped Econ 101, and had to get tutors for both of my math classes. To say I was a genius or whiz-kid would be far from the truth. But I had their contact details, and really what did I have to lose?

So, I picked up the phone and dialed Peter, the general manager at Solar World. The conversation went something like this:

Me: Hi, can I speak to Peter, please?

Peter: This is him. How can I help?

Me: Peter, my name is Shirley Morrison, and my friend, Josh Smith [the son of my parents' friend], recommended that I reach out to you. Do you have a minute to speak?

Peter: Yes, what is this about?

Me: Well, I am currently in college and interested in getting into the renewable energy industry. Josh told me about your company, and I did some research, and it's awe-inspiring! I wanted to see if you would have time to grab coffee with me next time I'm in San Francisco? Again, I'm in school and not graduating for nine months, but I just want to learn more about the renewable industry. Do you think you could spare thirty minutes to speak with me?

Peter: Of course, happy to help. When will you be in San Francisco next?

And that was it! Honestly, painless. Sure, it was a little awkward at first, but in the end, it was simple. You ask for help and start to build your network, however weak the connection seems at first.

One analogy that made me smile was equating it to *Finding Nemo* For example, in the movie, each animal does its part to assist Nemo's father to find Nemo. They assist him not because they have to, but because he asks for help, and typically when someone asks for help, you help them—it's naturally the right thing to do. And trust me, it comes around . . . one day you'll be the one getting a call from a university student asking for help.

You can also email if you don't have their number. However, remember that the average manager gets three hundred plus emails per day so it's easy to get lost in spam or overload. It's more powerful to call and follow up via email.

Rule of thumb: Phones are for conversations, and emails are for confirmations. If you find yourself writing an email, which seems more like a conversation with the other person—STOP—pick up the phone and make the call.

- In person/phone/Zoom = for conversations
- Email = for confirmations

You can leverage your existing network, family, friends, and own phonebook, talk to people about their job, and enter the industries you are interested in.

If I hadn't been able to get Peter over the phone, I could have sent an email like this:

Hi Peter,

Hope you are well.
My friend, Josh Smith, recommended I reach out to you. I am currently in UC Santa Barbara, but very interested in getting into renewable energy when I graduate in nine months. Would you have time for a Zoom call or coffee with me next week in San Francisco to discuss your experience in the renewable industry? I would really like to hear your perspective on the industry and any insights you can share.
I look forward to hearing back from you.

Kind regards,
Shirley

If it's a call or Zoom, follow these guidelines, which can be applied to any industry. Remember to be yourself and be natural, but feel free to have the question tips below in front of you if you get stuck. Most of these questions can be tailored to any situation: spend time going through these questions and adapting them to your situation.

Guidelines for your phone call or Zoom:

1. Explain your situation. Are you in college, graduating in nine months, and want to start talking to people in the respective industry? Or looking to make an industry change in the next nine months? Whatever your situation is, be open

with people. Be genuine and sincere about your position.

2. How is everything going in the industry? Lots of growth?

3. How did you get into the industry? Specific company?

4. Do you like it? What skills have you gained from your role?

5. What advice would you give someone like me looking to get into the field or industry?

6. Do you know of any companies that are looking to hire people in this field or industry?

7. Is there anyone else you could connect me with to learn more or would be potentially hiring in the next nine months?

8. Would you have availability next week or the following to meet for coffee in person to further discuss?

If it's a Zoom call, then remember these tips and to prepare beforehand. Check yourself and make sure to portray the image you want virtually.

KEY: Be genuine and honest about your current situation. Bring ENERGY and an eagerness to learn. I was excited and ambitious to be successful. You don't need to be the smartest in the room or the best in your class. Beat the smartest kid by being interested, prepared, and having a plan.

In addition to Peter, I reached out to several people in the financial services and technology industries. My parents are friends with Carrie Schwab, daughter of Charles Schwab, the Fortune 500 Company. The Charles Schwab Company was founded fifty years ago and is the third largest asset management company in the world, with revenue above $10 billion and employing over nineteen thousand people across the globe. I remember writing the email, which for all my embarrassment, is below. I think I looked over it a million times before sending it. Looking back, it makes me feel silly, but at the time, I was twenty-two, about to graduate, unconfident, and unsure of what I wanted from life.

> Hi Carrie,
>
> Hope you're well! I've heard fantastic things about you.
> My parents recommended I reach out to you. I am about to graduate college in nine months and start thinking about what I want to do after school. I was wondering if you would have time to meet with me next week or the following to discuss the financial industry?
> I look forward to hearing from you.
>
> Kind regards,
> Shirley

For all introductory emails: keep the emails short, clear, and to the point.

Carrie was kind enough to respond to my email and set up a time via her assistant to meet with me in a few weeks' time. To this day, I remember the Schwab office clearly. The building was in the middle of the Financial District in downtown San Francisco. It was the tallest and biggest building on the entire block. As you walked into the lobby, there was a security desk that took over half the room with the Schwab stamp in the middle.

I remember proudly saying to the security guard in the lobby, "I'm meeting with Carrie Schwab."

And he was like, "Why are you yelling?" I guess I was nervous.

I took the elevators up to one of the top floors. Carrie's secretary came out to greet me. I remember feeling very grownup and also so inexperienced at the same time as I sat down in a beautifully designed chair on top of white carpet. I remember asking myself, *Why am I here? I don't think I even want to work in financial services, but I can't rule it out, considering I have no job offers. Going from Global Studies Major to finance is definitely a jump!* All these thoughts in my head kept going round and round. And then the big kicker: *I hope Carrie likes me.* Ten minutes later, Carrie came out of her office and shook my hand.

Carrie Schwab was nothing like I'd expected. She made me feel comfortable within the first minute, telling me that her son was my age and that she loves working with young adults. She was very down to earth and relatable. *How can this high-powered woman be so naturally awesome? Wow.* The first question she had for me was, "How can I help you?"

I was honest.

"Carrie, I don't know what I want to do after I graduate, and I am starting to look at my options. Can you tell me about the financial services industry? Would you recommend someone like myself to get into the sector at this time?"

And then . . . I listened to what she had to say.

She was honest with me back and told me it was tough. She talked openly about her experiences and her time at Schwab, working with her dad, and her very successful career. I listened. I asked genuine questions that I wanted to learn.

"What's good about the financial services world?"

"What skills have you gained from working at Charles Schwab?"

"Do you hire graduates, or would a graduate need a different degree?"

"Who is your main competitor?"

After a good half hour of discussion, nearing almost the end of our forty-five minute talk, I finally said, "Carrie, do you know of anyone in your industry who is hiring that I could reach out to? Is there anyone you could introduce me to or connect me with?' Now this question allowed me to ask if Schwab was hiring indirectly, along with any other company that Carrie knew. Most likely, if the company is hiring, the person will let you know if you ask this question. So that's another tip: be subtle rather than desperate and direct.

She said, "Let me think about it." She then named three people she could connect me with off the top of her head. All of these people were doing well and working for good firms outside of Schwab. She connected me via email introductions thirty minutes after our meeting.

See one of the emails below . . .

Dear Shirley,

Please meet my good friend, Tom, from Wells Fargo. Tom is a business development executive in the Bay Area. There is not a person he doesn't know, and he is fantastic at building relationships. He is glad to meet with you to share his work and other potential ideas for your job seeking.

Tom, my dear—take care of Shirley!

to Carrie,

> *Carrie—Thank you for the introduction!!*
> *Hi Tom,*
>
> *Carrie spoke very highly of you. Thank you for*
> *agreeing to meet with me; I really appreciate it.*
> *Would you be available for a meeting sometime*
> *next week?*
> > *I look forward to speaking.*
>
> *Kind regards,*
> *Shirley*

The funny part about meeting with Carrie was that I decided not to pursue a career in financial services. Therefore, none of the contacts actually helped me with the job I chose, but they gave me something else. They gave me time to rehearse my pitch, practice having conversations with professionals, and help me think about my future. Everyone has something to offer you, something you can learn from. Take in what people say: LISTEN. And come to your own conclusions of what you want to do and what's best for you.

To be explicitly clear, not everyone has a densely networked friendship group that can offer assistance to develop a young person's career. You don't have to be lucky to use the advice in this book; instead think alternatively and outside of the box. Where can you go to build a network of your liking? Whether that's through your local church or YMCA, or even school. Are there clubs or associations you could join? Community committees where you can meet professionals? Nothing is off limits.

There was a famous story in the paper of a young teenager in England who grew up in the council estates. He had decided he wanted to be rich and literally googled, "richest area in London." He then went to this area in London and knocked on doors asking people how they made their money, trying to get career advice. A couple who opened their door were fascinated by this young, determined individual and helped him land his first job at a top finance firm.

Anyone from any background can use the advice in this book to help them go out and become their desired-future-self. Ask for the help. Ask for the introductions. ABOVE ALL, follow up with people. Write a handwritten thank-you note when someone takes the time to speak with you. If you don't have stationery, go out and buy some. It's rare to receive mail nowadays, and I can say from personal experience, a handwritten thank-you note has helped me land interviews and jobs. If they introduce you to someone via email, promptly follow up and reach out to the individual and go meet with them. Be your utmost professional self; do what you say you're going to do!

Thank-you notes should be genuine and short. Add in some information and make it personal. Here is an example:

Dear Carrie,

Thank you for meeting with me yesterday.
I am genuinely grateful for the insights you shared on your career and your experiences—I learned a lot. I also appreciate all the industry knowledge and introductions you made for me.

> *Thank you again for your help and coaching. I really appreciate it.*
>
> *Sincerely,*
> *Shirley*

When people stick their necks out for you, and you don't follow up, they will not help you again. By NOT following up with people, others lose trust in their relationships with you. Networks are built on trust. So put reminders in your diary to write that thank-you note afterward.

I have had countless people call me and say, "Can you tell me about your experience? How can I get a job at your company? What do I need to do?" I give them information and give them recommendations of things to do to get an interview, but I never hear from them again. No follow up. Occasionally, I'll get an email a few weeks or months later, asking to meet up again to further discuss. And I write back with, "Apologies, I am too busy." If I help someone, then what I am really doing is cultivating a business relationship in a 'what-goes-around-comes-around' philosophy. And if the other person doesn't get that, then not much is ever going to be coming back at me, and I would be better placed helping someone else, or just helping myself. While this is an organic and open-ended way of operating with no clear goals, it is how business (and indeed most things in life) work.

In comparison, interviewing is selling yourself. You're a salesperson and you're still selling yourself. The people you're meeting with should not have to follow up with you; you need to follow up with them. By following up, it shows that you care, are appreciative of people's time, and are interested in continuing the conversation. Sometimes the difference between following up and not following up is getting a JOB.

In summary: go out there and start networking. Reach out to people you normally wouldn't and prepare to have a discussion with them. Ask questions, and talk to people about what you are hoping to do in the future. Most importantly, follow-up after your Zoom or in-person meeting with your growing network and go buy stationery.

Suggestions of timely follow up:

- ✔ Write the thank-you note the same day as your meeting. It keeps the momentum going, and they should receive the note in one to two days.
- ✔ If they asked for more information, a follow-up email will suffice and should be sent the day after your in-person meeting.

ACTIVITY

Let's start to think about your own network. Where do you spend your time? For example, what groups or organizations are you involved with in your community? Could you cultivate contacts through your local church, through sports at the local YMCA, or maybe through your volunteering work with climate change? What about your LinkedIn and Instagram connections—maybe you can use the platforms to carefully seek the appropriate contacts to help steer your career?

Everyone has a network that can offer assistance for young individuals to develop a career to do whatever they like. It might not feel like it right away, but you don't know who your neighbors or church friends know until you ask. The following questions will start to prepare you for networking. Take time to really think through these questions, so you don't miss any opportunities once you get going.

Go through these and write down your answers:

1. Why are you networking?
2. What are you looking for in a potential job?
3. What type of people are you looking to network with? And why?
4. Who are the key people you want to get to know?
5. How do you intend to meet these people?
6. Can you call on your parents, schoolteachers, and friends' networks? Really think hard about your community and doors that can potentially open for you. Who knows you or your family? Remember sometimes a little "hello" can lead to great things.
7. Who do you know in your own network? Let's start with three people. Who are the three people you will reach out to first?
8. Do you have stationery? How's your handwriting? Thank-you notes are going to help you stay front of mind for people and aid in your networking.

Being genuinely interested in your job search is key to your future success. Follow what makes you passionate—when you follow your passion, success tends to be close behind.

Now let's go network and adapt these questions to your situation. The biggest hurdle is starting! Now you're talking to people and making it happen via phone, Zoom, or on email. You have started to build a professional network by being prepared and knowing your interest. Your "why."

CHAPTER 3

HOW TO APPLY FOR A JOB DURING COVID AND BEYOND

#HOW TO APPLY 4 A JOB TODAY

N ow it's time to decide which industry you want to pursue, and even more specifically, which companies. By this time you might have had multiple conversations with people in different industries and organizations, or plans for those conversations. You may be starting to get a feel for what you want to do and what industry you want to pursue (don't freak out if you still have no idea). The key to all of this—and some would say with life itself—is to go with your gut and your research. What do they combined tell you is the best option for you?

Make a list of the top five companies in the industry that you wish to join, even if you feel it may be a stretch— push your boundaries, because, why not? Do you know anyone at these companies? Do your new connections know anyone at these companies? Have you asked?

When I was looking for a job, after multiple conversations and talking to people in three different industries, I decided to pursue a role in the technology industry. I made a list of my top five technology companies that I would potentially like to join with the goal to get an interview with each one.

They were:

1. Salesforce
2. Oracle
3. Clarizen
4. Slack
5. AdRoll

I had already had the initial interviews at numbers three and four, which were both start-ups, but I really wanted to get into a larger corporation. My gut told me to go for a position at Oracle. At the time, I literally had no idea what Oracle did, but I did my research and learned that it was one of the top sales companies in the world. Oracle had a strong brand and reputation on the market as a leader in the technology industry. Combining my gut and my research, I decided that was where I wanted to work.

Reviewing my connections on LinkedIn, it became pretty apparent that I knew absolutely no one at Oracle. However, I had a friend from university named Scott who was connected to a guy that worked at Oracle named Michael, who also went to our university. So I had a distant connection to an Oracle employee through my university friend. To be honest, I had not spoken to Scott for at least a year as he was a year ahead of me in university. Would he even remember me? Or be willing to help me?

That's when I remembered a quote I had heard years ago, "A simple HELLO could lead to a million things."

I decided I had nothing to lose and wrote to Scott on LinkedIn to see how well he knew Michael at Oracle:

Hi Scott,

Hope all is well with you!
I wanted to ask you a huge favor . . . How
well do you know Michael from Oracle? I am
very interested in getting a job at Oracle. Any
chance you would feel comfortable making an
introduction? Would be great to pick his brain
about the company, etc. . . .
As per usual, I'll owe you a beer for this . . . ;)

Best,
Shirley

Scott wrote back the next day:

Shirley,
No problem at all. Actually, I know Michael
very well! We were in the same Fraternity at our
University. Will make an introduction for you
shortly. Good luck with your search!!
I look forward to that beer . . .

Best,
Scott

Scott proceeded to make an introduction for me to Michael over LinkedIn. I asked to have a call with Michael as he only worked at Oracle as a salesperson and was not a hiring manager. He agreed. The following week, we had a call where we discussed the company and environment—all that seemed to be exactly what I was looking for:

- Top training programs for employees

- High earning potential
- Working large multi-million-dollar deals
- International company
- Fun and young culture environment

I was getting really excited on the call. Michael talked to me about his experience and how he was enjoying Oracle. As a person, I am not afraid of being direct and asking for what I want, as I have found that I often succeed when doing it. So close to the end of the call, I asked him point-blank, "Michael, Oracle seems like a great company. Thanks for all the information. I would be really interested in applying for a role. Do you know of any teams that are looking to hire or could you put me in touch with a hiring manager at Oracle?"

He said to send my résumé to him, and he could give it to one of the hiring managers. I thanked him repeatedly and promised him a coffee for his help. He said not to worry and that he was always happy to help a fellow Gaucho (mascot for UCSB), but no promises as he wasn't sure if Oracle was hiring or not at the moment. But I would at least have a conversation with management.

After the call, I got out my stationery and wrote Michael a thank-you note. A day after my call with Michael, I followed up and sent him my résumé, as well as thanked him again for his time and for his help. A week went by, and I heard nothing. I decided to send Michael a pleasant reminder and check-in via email.

Hi Michael,

Hope all is well.
Thanks again for speaking with me last week. Just

wanted to check-in and see if you had any feedback from your management?

Talk soon,
Shirley

I didn't want to seem too eager, and I also didn't want to annoy him. There is a fine line between being pleasantly persistent and being annoying. You've got to keep in mind that this person's job is not to find you a job.

A day after my reminder email, I received a phone call from a hiring manager at Oracle. He asked if I could come in for a formal interview the following week.

WOW.

Now, this story may not seem typical, but it's not unusual. I used my network, even if it was a stretch at first, to make a connection happen. I reached out to a "friend" who was really more of an acquaintance and asked to be introduced to his friend—who for all I know may have also been more of an acquaintance to him. I was pleasantly persistent with my contacts and followed up in a timely manner, which eventually resulted in an interview at my desired company.

Activity: Build Your Résumé/CV to Help You Get Your Foot in the Door

Write down five companies that you would like to apply to for an interview. Start to see who you know there or who your friends know at these companies. ASK around. Are they hiring? Would your friend of a friend be open to speaking with you?

How can you get your foot in the door?

From my experience, sending your résumé in cold without a warm introduction does not end in getting the interview. Companies legally have to place ads online for open roles even if they have decided to hire internally. Be wary of wasting your time sending in applications for roles you find online. I'm not saying don't do it, but rather that my own experience tells me that finding a champion in the desired company is more likely to yield an interview than sending in your résumé cold.

At some companies, especially the most well-known and extreme cases, 85 percent of new hires come from referrals, leaving only 15 percent being from jobs posted online and/or from other sources. The saying, "it's not what you know, but who you know" is one of the foundations in our society; its significance continues to dominate the workplace in the twenty-first century and probably also the foreseeable future. While keeping this phrase in mind, be cautious of wasting your time applying online and spend more time meeting/connecting with people at your desired companies.

Additionally, a résumé is KEY to getting an interview. Make sure your résumé is up-to-date and has the appropriate information to secure you an interview. What is the job description? Have you tied that specific description to your résumé? Make sure you are changing and tweaking your résumé for each role for which you apply. I have found that many of my friends update their résumé once and then send it out for many different jobs/roles, which does not get them the interview. By "tweaking," I mean adding/changing the language in your CV so that it is relevant by looking at the specific job description and then modifying your CV to match the requirements (please note that résumés and CV are the same thing and terms

I will use interchangeably). Let's say the job description is looking for a candidate who is: "A marketing expert with experience collaborating with sales teams; helping to increase revenue growth and market reach. Ambitious, personable, and driven individual to join a fast-paced team and company."

Here is an example of tweaking the above description to your résumé:

- ✔ Focused on increasing sales through marketing by collaborating closely with other lines of the business—strategically aligned to sales team
- ✔ Highly self-motivated; determined to understand the business need and develop strategy with channel partners and focused on the success of the team
- ✔ Takes initiative and routinely communicates; works well in a fast-paced environment

Again, if you really want the job, or even just to get the interview, take the time to update your résumé for each role. Your résumé should tell a story about how you are the right fit for that specific job/role, and each one will likely be slightly different.

From living aboard, I have firsthand experience with different résumé/CV expectations depending on the country/location of the job. In the United States, a résumé/CV in most cases should be one page, unless you have ten plus years of experience, and then you may have two pages. However, many people like my dad (now retired) had a one-page résumé up until the day he handed in his notice after forty years of being in the workforce. Please note that if you do decide to submit a résumé longer than one page, it needs to be one or two pages. Not 1.5, which will leave too much empty space and can make your application look unprofessional. My advice: keep it clean and precise and summarize your relevant skills in one page. Have your LinkedIn profile be a more extensive CV, knowing that your potential employer will check you out and verify the details.

Now, in the United Kingdom it's a completely different story. I've had UK bosses tell me that they would never even consider a candidate unless their résumé/CV was two pages in length, at least! Take into consideration where you are in the world, and where you want to apply globally. If it is another country, then you will need to look into what a typical résumé/CV format would look like from their country. For example, in Scandinavian countries it is normal to add a photo of yourself to your CV/résumé. Assuming you are applying abroad, the company will take into account the fact that you are a foreigner, so you are not expected to know all the rules. However, don't you want to show that you can adapt to their culture? Don't you want to prove that you want to do things in the correct cultural way as they see it locally, therefore showing your adaptability?

My suggestion is for you to focus on using the following checklist for your CV/résumé and make it the main way (along with the internal champion you found) to get your foot in the door with the desired company. If you feel that a cover letter is necessary as well, then use the following also for details on how to write a great cover letter.

Activity

Here are some résumés and sample letters. This activity is to turn your own CV/résumé into something similar to what I have that follows. In other words, beef up the words you already have to make it look like something more. Feel free to use the form of these CV/résumés, which can be downloaded off my website: www.samorrison.com.

US Résumé Format Checklist

Your resume is a *marketing document* that showcases your value proposition. Its main objective *is to sell you.* It is forward looking and highlights your relevant accomplishments and transferable skills. It is NOT a laundry list of your previous responsibilities.

Good to note: This résumé is targeted toward a corporate role. If applying for a start-up or more creative field, then there is likely more flexibility to be unconventional.

____ My résumé is ONE page only (no exceptions)

____ All of my margins are a minimum of 0.5"

____ I only used fonts Times New Roman, Calibri, or Arial

____ My font is a minimum of 10 pt. and maximum of 12 pt. (including name and contact information)

____ I did not overuse *italics*, underlines, or **bold**

____ I have sufficient white space

____ My section headers are written like this and in this order:

EXPERIENCE
EDUCATION
ADDITIONAL (this section is optional, but highly recommended)

____ My contact information—name, address (optional), phone, email—is centered at the top of the résumé

____ I varied my verbs at the beginning of each bullet

____ My dates and locations are right-justified; all dates on right-side margins (left, center, right)

____ My dates are in reverse chronological order; i.e. you want to put your most recent experience at the top of the page

---

YOUR NAME
Phone *(Required)* | first.last.20##@gmail.com *(Required)*
LinkedIn URL *(Optional)*

EXPERIENCE

MOST RECENT COMPANY/ORGANIZATION
(One line italics descriptor of company if not as known)   Location(s) of Office

Title A   Dates of Employment
- Supervised a team of . . . . more . . . . and executed the 2-month project . . . .
. . . . . more . . . . more . . . . resulting in new projects from clients worth over
$M . . . .
- Re-negotiated contracts with vendors worth over $MM . . . . more . . . .
more . . . . which led to XX% increased profits YOY
- Developed new marketing strategy and implemented . . . . more . . . . increasing
market share by XX% . . .
- Other great things you have done . . . . more . . . . more . . . .
. . . .

Title B   Dates of Employment
- Established new processes . . . . more . . . . more . . . .
reducing downtime by XX% more . . . . more . . . . more . . . .
. . . .
- Led a team of . . . . . in designing and executing . . . . more . . . .
more . . . . cutting costs by XX%
- Identified . . . more . . . . . . and presented solutions to client's senior management . . . .
more . . . . resulting in additional engagements worth $XXX,000 over 6 months . . . .

Title C   Dates of Employment
- Analyzed . . . and presented to senior management . . . implemented . . . . more . . . .
. . . . resulting in . . . . more . . . which will be implement in fall of 20## . . . .
- Managed team of . . . . more . . . . more . . . increasing revenue by
XX% . . . more . . . . more . . . .
- Other great things you did during the summer internship . . . .

NEXT RECENT COMPANY/ORGANIZATION 2   Location(s) of Office
Title   Dates of Employment
- Researched and developed . . . more . . . . more . . . . resulting in
first year revenues of $XXX,000
- Collaborated with . . . . more . . . . more . . . .
exceeding goals by XX%
- Created . . . more . . . . more . . . . increasing productivity by XX%

EDUCATION
_____

UCLA ANDERSON SCHOOL OF MANAGEMENT   Los Angeles, CA
MBA, Full-Time Program, Specialization, XXX GMAT *(if 720+ and valued by your desired industry)*
                                                            June 20##
- Honors: . . . . more . . . . more . . . . more . . . .
  . . . .
- Leadership: . . . . more . . . . more . . . . more . . . .
  . . . .
- Membership: . . . . more . . . . more . . . .
  . . . . more . . . . more . . . .

YOUR UNDERGRADUATE UNIVERSITY   Location
BA (or equivalent), Major/Minor, X.XX GPA *(if higher than or equal to 3.5, the Anderson average)*
                                                         Graduation Date
- Honors: . . . . more . . . . more . . . . more . . . .
  . . . .
- Leadership: . . . . more . . . . more . . . . more . . . . .
  . . . .
- Membership: . . . . more . . . . more . . . . more . . .
  . . . .
  and other relevant information about your undergraduate education

ADDITIONAL *(this section is optional, but recommended—especially if it's interesting)*
_____

- Certifications: CFA, Series 63, ARGUS, Six Sigma Black Belt . . .
- Languages: Spanish, Farsi . . .
- Software: Java, Google Analytics, C/C++ . . .
- Volunteer Work: . . . Memberships . . .
- Interests: Other interesting things that would start a conversation or demonstrate your interest in your target industry/function

UK Résumé Format Checklist

Your résumé is a *marketing document* that showcases your value proposition. Its main objective *is to sell you*. It is forward looking and highlights your relevant accomplishments and transferable skills. It is NOT a laundry list of your previous responsibilities.

_____ My résumé is TWO pages (as a recent graduate ONE page is acceptable as well)

_____ All of my margins are a minimum of 0.5"

_____ I only used fonts Times New Roman, Calibri, or Arial

_____ My font is a minimum of 10 pt. and maximum of 12 pt. (including name and contact information)

_____ I did not overuse _italics_, <u>underlines</u>, or **bold**

_____ I have sufficient white space

_____ My section headers are written as below and in this order:

PROFILE AND SKILLS PROFILE _(Different format than a US Résumé*)_

- **Profile:** A hundred words at the top of the résumé outlining your characteristics and past work experience, along with your qualities and attributes as a person. It's short and sweet, but gives a few sentences on the professional you are and will aspire to be for the perspective employer.

- **Skills profile:** shows the prospective employer your soft and hard skills. Soft skills are hard to quantify; e.g. leadership, professional attitude, work ethic, etc. While hard skills are typically required for the job; e.g. analyzing data and being able to code, knowing how to build a house, design architecture, create financial reports, etc. Both are hugely important to have in your résumé because your employer is looking to hire someone based on their skills!

WORK EXPERIENCE

EDUCATION

ACCOMPLISHMENTS/LANGUAGES _(this section is optional, but highly recommended)_

_____ My contact information—name, address (optional), phone, email—is centered at the top of the résumé

_____ I varied my verbs at the beginning of each bullet

_____ My dates and locations are right-justified; all dates on right side margins (left, center, right)

_____ My dates are in reverse chronological order; i.e. you want to put your most recent experience at the top of the page

*Next is an example of the CV I used to successfully apply to Salesforce in the United Kingdom.

YOUR NAME

Phone number *(required)* | Morrisonshirley452@gmail.com

Linkedin URL *(optional)*

Profile

A confident and highly organized _____ professional with the ability to adapt to a fast-paced work environment. As a recent graduate with honors from _____, leading by example was part of the curriculum, along with _____. Fast learner with a 'can-do' attitude, always working towards finding the right solution for everyone. Dedicated leader in ____ with over ____ years of experience. My achievements include _____, delivering _____ for ____ across a ___ business. Directly responsible for _____. Strong experience in analyzing financial reports, building spreadsheets _____.

Skills Profile

Leadership
- Natural leader with the ability to adapt to new cultures, complex product sets and industries
- Takes initiative to understand other people's perspective and focused on the success of the team

Motivation and Ambition
- Aspirations to continue to lead a sales team, and sell complex technology to corporations around the world
- Highly self-motivated and competitive; additionally, collaborative and team-oriented
- Consistently prospect and drive new business while managing current deals
- Determined to find the right solutions for the customer, and understand the business need

Communication, Presentation and Networking
- Cultivate relationships with C-level executives and key decision makers. Ability to find, drive and close complex sales cycles
- Maintain frequent, open communication with customers with whom there are no active deals
- Routinely communicate and update forecast to management accurately

Innovation and Problem-Solving
- Continually evaluate industry and customer changes to adapt sales techniques (messaging, communication methods, and campaigns)
- Always develop and evaluate multiple solutions to a problem until resolution—can't leave a problem unsolved; works until we solved the issue and everyone walks away happy

Work Experience

AFINITI Applies AI to predict behavior and pair better   London, United Kingdom

Director, Client Services   Feb 2018—Present
Responsible for business development team and sales execution in the UK
- Key Account Director for the largest telecommunication provider in the UK
- Managing a team of 4 Business Development Consultants—sales training/mentoring companywide
- Successfully qualified, negotiated, and will close the first ever collections deal in the company—£5M
- Working closely with AI technology team to enterprise complex models, technology and value of the go-to-market
- Leading the largest enterprise opportunity to date and on target to close in 2019 Q2

ORACLE CORPORATION   London UK/Redwood Shores, California

Lead Account Manager—United Kingdom   June 2016—Jan 2018
Direct responsibility for key account sales to CTOs, CIOs, and CEOs
- Earned promotion to 'Lead Account Manager' team within 15 months of being in UK out of interview pool of 20 internal candidates
- Received the Top performer award in FY17 H2 for Retail Accounts
- Closed £1M which was the largest Oracle cloud deal in all of Retail Accounts for H2
- Through Fiscal Q3'17, lead all UK sales quota programs and was a candidate for Oracle President Club/Travel for FY17; Also, one of the youngest people in role in United Kingdom/Europe

Investment Accounts, Field Sales – United Kingdom   November 2014 – May 2016
- Was chosen from ~30 international candidates to move from SF Headquarters to UK field sales team
- Exceed annual quota, 108% in FY16
- Exceed annual quota, 137% in FY15
- Received Top Performer award for all of Investment Accounts for FY15

Account Manager, Sales – Northern California   September 2013 – Oct 2014
- My team closed the biggest Q4 deal in NorCal of FY14 with SuccessFactors at $75M, found the 'mole'
- Exceeded annual quota, 110% of FY14 annual budget
- Received Top Performer award for all of National West in Q3
- Mentoring new hires, leading the team in appoints, call status and positive attitude

GESTAMP ASETYM SOLAR   San Francisco, California

Business Development Manager, Sales – Solar Power plants – North America   March 2011 – August 2013
- Started in entry Sales; promoted to Business Development Manager in ~9 months after starting at firm
- Extensive US and European HQ visits to develop solid pipeline of business prospects. Developed and closed deals that met for new business of $3 Million in project revenues; on target for ~50% increase in goal 2013

Education

UNIVERSITY OF CALIFORNIA, SANTA BARBARA   Santa Barbara, California
Bachelor degree in Global Studies (Business focus)   Graduated June 2011
- Major GPA: 3.5/4.0
- Relevant Coursework: Internal Relations, Business Economics, and Global Processes
UNIVERSITAT AUTONOMA DE BARCELONA   Barcelona, Spain
International Relations-Global business (12-month full Spanish emersion program) June '09 - June '10

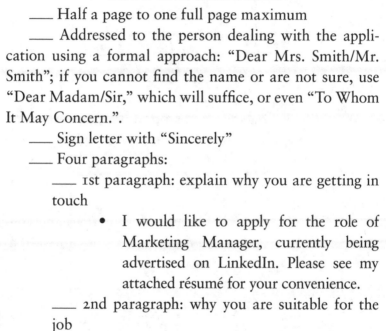

- Major GPA: 3.7/4.0
- Relevant Coursework: Strategic Global Behavior in Business/Economics

Accomplishments/ Languages

High-school captain for basketball and soccer teams (3 years each), Vice President of student body, played Lacrosse competitively for UCSB and led a fundraising campaign for Junior League of London; reads, writes and speaks in Spanish. Ran the London Marathon back in 2016, currently learning French and an avid CrossFit goer.

US/UK Cover Letter Format

____ Half a page to one full page maximum

____ Addressed to the person dealing with the application using a formal approach: "Dear Mrs. Smith/Mr. Smith"; if you cannot find the name or are not sure, use "Dear Madam/Sir," which will suffice, or even "To Whom It May Concern.".

____ Sign letter with "Sincerely"

____ Four paragraphs:

____ 1st paragraph: explain why you are getting in touch

- I would like to apply for the role of Marketing Manager, currently being advertised on LinkedIn. Please see my attached résumé for your convenience.

____ 2nd paragraph: why you are suitable for the job

- As you can see from my attached résumé, I have studied communications at University of Birmingham for the last four years, along with experience working at the top marketing agency, Flower Me. I believe the knowledge and skills I have built up over this time would make me a perfect candidate for the role.

____ 3rd paragraph: what you can do for the company

- In my current role as Marketing Associate at Flower Me, I have been responsible for year on year growth, increasing our B2B product lines by 125 percent in under six months, which helped increase the company bottom line by 30 percent in revenue.

____ 4th paragraph: reiterate and summarize

- I am confident that I could bring this level of success to your company and help build upon your strong reputation as one of the top Marketing agencies in the UK. With my previous experience and expertise, I believe I can start actively contributing to the business as soon as possible.

  Thank you for your time and consideration for the role. I look forward to hearing from you.

Below is an example of the cover letter I used when I was applying for roles in London. I ended up going with Salesforce instead of Google, but it did land me a conversation with the Google recruitment team and an in-person discussion.

To Whom It May Concern,

I wish to apply for the role of Field Sales Representative, Google Cloud–London, currently being advertised. Please find enclosed my CV for your consideration.

As you can see from my attached CV, I have over seven years' experience in sales, and I believe the knowledge and skills built up during this time make me the perfect candidate for the role.

In my current role as Director, Client Services at Afiniti, I have been responsible for AI sales for existing customers and new business—about to close the first ever collections deal in the company (£5M). In my previous role with Oracle, I never missed my annual target four years in a row) and closed the largest cloud deal in FY17 Q2 for Retail Accounts.

I am confident that I can bring this level of success with me to your company and help Google build upon their reputation. With my previous experience and expertise in selling cloud products, I believe I can start actively contributing to the business as soon as possible.

Thank you for your time and consideration. I look forward to meeting with you to discuss my application further.

Kind regards,
Shirley Morrison

CHAPTER 4

HOW TO NAIL THE INTERVIEW VIRTUALLY

#NAIL THE INTERVIEW VIRTUALLY

Job interviews are like first dates.
Good impressions count.
Awkwardness can occur.
Outcomes are unpredictable.

GOAL: Aim for the interviewer (the person hosting the interview) to speak 85 percent of the time and the interviewee (that would be you) to speak 15 percent of the time. Studies show that it is more than likely, if you follow this guideline, that you will get the job!

People like to hear their own voice. I know, hardly a breakthrough piece of information. But we all seem to forget it all the time—perhaps because we're too busy talking.

Studies show that when party number one speaks the majority of the time to party number two throughout a conversation, then party number one walks away saying how great party number two is. Ask party number one anything about party number two and they would have nothing to say, except how much they really like party number two. Sounds stupid, I know, but it works. Now you might ask: so how do I get them to speak the majority of the time?

That is where I can help. Whenever I go into an interview, I do the following:

Number one and hopefully obvious to everyone, I LOOK THEM UP ON LINKEDIN. If you don't have a LinkedIn profile, get on it immediately. LinkedIn is your public résumé, like Instagram for the professional world. Nearly everyone has a LinkedIn profile. If you can't seem to find them on LinkedIn, then you're likely not spelling their name correctly. So try again. Find them and try to understand a bit about them. Can you find any connections? Do you have any similar interests? How long have they been at the company? What is their background? Have they written any publications or any posts? (If so, read them.) To be clear, you don't want to be a stalker, but you want to try to get to know your audience. What type of person are they?

The second thing I do is get down my answers to basic interview questions because, in any interview, you tend to get similar questions. For example, why should I hire you? Why are you interested in working at this specific company?

These questions are short and sweet, but if you're not prepared with a practiced answer, then they can leave you speechless or make you sound incoherent. I call them "elbowers" because you can get winded by them and then it's hard to come back from that. So I prepare by writing out a list of questions that the interviewer may ask me and then figuring out potential answers to these questions. I don't memorize this list, but I do prepare myself by knowing how I would answer these types of questions and then practice by answering out loud.

Here's a tip: What you've written may sound eloquent and fabulous inside your head, but when you say it out loud, you can sometimes get tongue-tied. Practicing your answers aloud will help you gain confidence and rhythm for the real interview. Ideally, if a friend, partner, or family member can go through the questions with you, all the better!

Next is a list of potential interview questions. These questions and answers seem like a "duh," but trust me: you can easily get an "elbower" during an interview if you don't think ahead, write your answers down, and practice saying them aloud. The best part about these general questions and answers is that they can be easily tweaked or changed for each company. Once you have your potential answers list written down, you can make subtle changes for each of your interviews.

Interview Sample Questions	Potential Answers	Additional Prompts to Help You Think Through Your Answers
Tell me about yourself.	I am the eldest of four; leading the family. I have been blessed to have a very international background, living all over the world in Australia, Indonesia, and Barcelona. Moving a lot as a kid really helped to develop my people skills. Over the last year I have been developing my sales skills and strategies at my current internship, while also studying at university.	Give some personality! Be yourself and talk about the individual you are outside of work.

(Continued on next page)

What is your background?	My background is sales; basically, finding new leads, developing a relationship, and executing on deals. Always looking to close. I've learned during my internship that I enjoy working with peoplem which is key for me and something I want to continue to do in my career.	What did you study that is valuable for this job? Or what internships in the past have you had that are relevant for this position?
Why do you want to work for us?	Oracle is an industry leader. Cloud offerings are very competitive in the industry and you need a strong brand, which Oracle has. I want to be where things are developing, changing, and growing. And I want to make a meaningful contribution to that development and growth. Additionally, I have friends at Oracle and they have talked about the strong team environment and leadership presence, plus the top-rated training program, which as I start out in my career is really important to me.	Be honest; what are the benefits of working for this company? Why are you interested to work there? What would you gain from working there?

One of my favorite interview questions is: Why do you want to work for us?

Such a classic interview question has so many potential answers. To answer it, think about what is driving you to look for a job in that industry, in that company. Why do you think the interviewer joined? Could you also be joining for the same reason?

Writing down these answers also helps you with your own process of understanding what you are looking for in your career and which company best suits your needs. Remember just as much as you are using them (for money, further training, their branding, etc.), they will be using you (working long hours, helping them increase revenues, pursue more clients, etc.). It's your life. The goal is not to just be employed; it's to be fulfilled and happy as you build your career, and starting out on the career ladder is just one step. Think about what it is you want back from the company.

They may even try to ask some deeper questions to see if you're a real human being. People like people who are genuine and honest, but who do not put all their weaknesses on the table. Don't just use work examples; talk about appropriate things in your personal life as well. They are trying to get to know you and understand your values as a person to see if you're a cultural fit for the company. Before the interview, ask yourself: Do you know the company values? Maybe it's trust? Honesty? Hard work? Never giving up until the problem is solved? How could you show an example of this in your own life?

See sample questions and answers next.

Interview Sample Questions	Potential Answers	Additional Prompts to Help You Think Through Your Answers
Can you give an example of a hardship you had to overcome?	As a freshman, I made the varsity soccer team, which is quite unusual as it normally is only girls in their last two years of high school, not their first (basically skipped three levels). That year there were four of us freshman that made the varsity soccer team. Now the following year, I walked up to the field for try outs assuming I would make the team again.	What's a hardship that shows your determination in life? Maybe a story from your childhood, your internship, or life in general? What is one of your most courageous memories that stands out for you?

(Continued on next page)

	My three other fellow friends were not so sure and communicated that they thought we could potentially lose our spots on the varsity team. And guess what? All three made the varsity team, except me. I was demoted to the junior team my second year. Now, I could have quit soccer, as it was quite embarrassing, or I could play my heart out and try again the following year. I decided to play my heart out and scored thirteen goals that year (we only play ten games a season). I was named Player of the Year and am still in the "hall of fame" for most goals scored on the junior team. The following year, I tried out for the varsity team and made it. It might seem silly, but this lesson taught me to never take anything for granted and you can overcome anything through grit and hard work.	It can be anything . . . Take a moment and write down something you have overcome.
What are your achievements?	Running a half marathon in under two hours. Starting out as the worst Spanish-speaker in my class to conquering the language and studying abroad for one year in university. Getting accepted into UCSB, which was my first choice of school and graduating with honors.	What are you most proud of? Sports? Your studies? Climbing a mountain? Competition in a competition? Get creative and have fun with this answer!

For many people, the hardest part of an interview is usually the questions around why they should hire you. This is the part where you need to really sell yourself. If you flip the question, what the interviewer is really asking is: what will I get in return if I bring you aboard at this company? The answer needs to stand out and impress your interviewer. When you answer this question, take your time, talk slowly, and really drive the "WHY YOU" home.

Here are some example questions and answers.

Interview Sample Questions	Potential Answers	Additional Prompts to Help You Think Through Your Answers
What are your three strengths and weaknesses?	I don't really like to flat-out talk about myself, but I think if you asked my peers my three strengths they would say are a driven individual—when I say I'm going to do something I get it done—excellent communicator, and thirdly I'm a people's person. WEAKNESSES: I am a hard worker and sometimes work too hard; need to learn how to delegate more. Not very good at doing my expenses. Sometimes I can be a perfectionist and want everything done right the first time; can be too helpful.	This is an old-school question; and its typically received with a non-genuine answer. As you really don't want to sit there and list all your weaknesses. Instead list qualities that are actually good attributes, but could be regarded as weaknesses.
Why should I hire you?	You should hire me because I'm dependable. I'm a hardworker and always do what I say. I was top of my class at university, while also working in sales; never missing my target during the twelve-month internship. I am confident that I can bring this level of success with me to your company and help Oracle build upon their reputation. I am reliable	What will the company get in return by bringing you on board? Will you be their top performer? Will you help generate more revenue? Help increase operational efficiencies?

(Continued on next page)

	and eager to learn new things. Additionally, I have a positive work attitude, I enjoying interacting with people, especially when there is a need to solve a problem. I am highly self-motivated and very teachable. Moreover I am a fast learner and eager to learn new things.	
Where do you see yourself in ten years?	I see myself as a leader in the industry. I am stimulated by the quality of my work, and can be recognized as an expert in my area, and I will be working with colleagues whom I like and respect. I see that potential here.	For this one, reach for the stars, but try to keep it more general as you don't want to pigeon-hole yourself into anything.

Create a list questions to ask the interviewer during the interview. For the actual interview, I like to go in with questions I have handwritten down for the interviewer. I try not to pull out my questions until the interviewer says, "Do you have any questions?" I've heard point-blank from managers that they won't hire people who "don't have any questions." If you start to think of an interview as a conversation, then you most definitely would have questions to keep the conversation going and interesting for all parties involved.

I cringe when I hear people say they have an interview and have to "present" to the panel or interviewer. Never make a presentation as part of an interview—only have conversations. If the company does ask you to give a formal presentation as part of your interview, make sure to stop and ask, "Am I on track?" during the presentation. "What would you do here?" Or "Is this what you expected?" Again, bring it back to having a conversation and avoid straight presenting by involving your audience.

Please see these questions that can help you for your next interview:

1. Are there monthly, daily, and/or yearly KPIs (Key Performance Indicators) for the role? If so, what are they? If it's a manager position: How do you help your team reach those KPIs/goals?
2. What incentives do you have for the top performers?
3. Can you touch on the training for the position?
4. How is the culture at your company? Competitive? Team oriented?
5. Who would be managing my team? How large are the teams? Are we broken up into industries and/or geographic regions?
6. Is there room for growth/advancement in my division? Typically, how long does someone work in the department before they are promoted to a management role?
7. What are the qualities your best employees possess? What are you looking for in a candidate?
8. What advice would you give someone like me looking to enter into this industry or even just this company?
9. Who are your competitors? If a potential customer is using your competitors, how do you engage them and sell them on your firm? What are the differentiators at this company compared to the competitors?
10. In two years from now, if I'm doing well, how much money would I be making? Can you give me a range?

The KEY is not only to ask questions, but to also get the interviewer talking about themselves. A lot of people forget this . . . Remember the goal—if you speak only 15 percent of the time and they speak 85 percent of the time . . . YOU LIKELY GET THE JOB.

Finally, make sure to ask the personal questions, which I tend to leave for the end of the interview. Again, these questions are to get the person talking about themselves, but it also gives you insight into the company. I've had people interviewing me tell me, "I'll probably leave in the next year . . . " And I'm like, "Well, if you're leaving, why the heck would I join?" Sometimes people can give you a huge insight into the company without really meaning to . . . so, listen.

These personal questions will also allow you to gauge whether the person really believes in the company or not. Choosing a company is like entering into a relationship. Sure, you can break up, but then you have to start dating again . . . So, find a "relationship" that really works for you. Do your research.

Personal Questions to Ask the Interviewer During the Interview

1. Where were you before this company?
2. What attracted you to this company?
3. What skills have you gained from this job?
4. What are your long-term goals here?
5. Where do you see the company in five years? Do you see yourself at the firm in five years?

All of these questions are essential for your interview, but there is one last question which is imperative to your success, which is: to ask for the job. This should be your final question before the end of the interview. I remember thinking how inappropriate the question was when I was told to ask for the job—thinking they would think I was being really pushy or aggressive if I asked for the job. However, it's quite the opposite in the working world. If you don't ask for the job, you greatly lessen your chances of getting it. They want to hire someone who really wants the job. So, ask for the job!

Most Important Question to Ask During the Interview

6. How did I do? Is there anything else I need to do to get hired by you? What else do I need to do or show to get hired by you? (You can give a cheeky smile as you say this, but definitely ask it!)

Another tip that has helped me stand out from the crowd is to do a "training day." After the interview, I ask the interviewer if it would be possible to come in for a day or a few hours to see what it's like during a typical day at the office. Work side-by-side with someone who has a similar role for a few hours. Talk to the team, and get a feeling for the culture/vibe. Or do a "training day" with their best employee and/or meet a few customers who are using the products or services. Again, this can give you a better insight into the environment and company. Plus, it shows the hiring manager you are taking this interview process seriously and are very interested in the role.

Now let's go back to my interview.

So, now I'd prepared for the interview by working on my "elbowers" out loud, wrote down my questions for the interviewer, and was ready for the interview with Oracle.

Thanks to my distant connection with Michael, who helped me land the job interview, I had a meeting with Donald, a director at Oracle. Here are a few things I learned about Donald through my research on LinkedIn.

- He had worked at Oracle for four years, starting as a rep and working his way up to a management role.
- He was an alumnus of Saint Mary's University.
- He was in several baseball groups on LinkedIn and had played baseball for Saint Mary's.

So, I had some background on him, but what type of person was he? How could I get inside information on Donald? Interviewing is very difficult, especially when you don't know your audience. How could I get to know my audience?

Answer: Use your resources. I decided to call Michael (my new acquaintance) and see what information I could get from him to better understand Donald. He explained:

- Donald was a relatively new manager;
- He was the youngest manager on the floor and was eager to prove himself;
- He was from somewhere in the Bay Area;
- He played a sport for his university; and
- He was recently engaged.

This additional information means I had an informal conversation about sports and growing up in the Bay Area. Be interested in the person interviewing you; however, the key here is to be genuine. No one likes it when you seem fake, so find something that genuinely interests you about them or find a similar interest. If you or they don't like sports or you couldn't find anything on their LinkedIn to relate to them, that's fine, but you can still try to get inside information on their personality or style. If you can show even the slightest bit of research and that you have gone out of your way to prep for an interview, it could land you the job.

Before the interview, I went through my basic questions and answers, changing them to Oracle specific language.

Walking into Oracle that day, I was excited and a bit nervous, but I was well prepared, knew my audience, and was ready to see if Oracle was a good fit for me. As much as they were interviewing me, I was ready and prepped to interview them.

Me: Hi, Donald, nice to meet you.
Donald: Shirley, welcome. Thanks for coming.
Me: I saw you're a Saint Mary's guy . . . I'm a Bay Area kid myself. Are you from the Bay Area originally?
Donald: Yes, born and raised.
Me: Me too! Where specifically?

The conversation continued. We were from similar areas; our high schools competed in sports again each other. I was a big athlete in high school and university, so for me talking sports is genuine.

Me: I saw you played baseball for Saint Mary's. I also played for my school and miss playing sports. Did you play all four years?
Donald: Yes, I played baseball. What sport did you play?

OK, so we connected on sports, which was not necessarily going to land me the job, but it helped to get the conversation going and for me to feel at ease with my interviewer. Additionally, it showed that I'd done my research and looked him up online.

People like people who are similar to them. It's a human instinct to like someone else who mirrors your physical and mental self. So finding common ground with someone can only increase your odds that they will like you more. It also helps you to relax in stressful environments (interviewing) and helps to ease the tension all around. If you do happen to be different or opposite from the interviewer (age, ethnicity, etc.), talk about something you love or are passionate about in the interview, if you have a moment. You never know when you will find a connection with someone else. And if not, at least they now know your passions and it will hopefully make for a nice conversation.

> **Donald:** Shirley, tell me about yourself.
> **Me:** Well, I'm the oldest of four, lived around the world. And I'm actually interested in living abroad eventually, which is why I have only been applying to international companies.
> **Donald (interrupts):** Which companies?
> **Me:** I'd rather not say, but they are direct competitors of Oracle. I actually already have an offer from one, but wanted to speak with Oracle before I make a decision.
> **Donald:** Interesting . . .

Side note: It's fine to let your interviewer know you are interviewing elsewhere—because you're interviewing them as much as they're interviewing you. You don't have to say the names of the companies. I've found people want someone who is getting offers elsewhere, too—people want to hire the best and the best tend to have multiple jobs offers.

Donald led the discussion and asked me several questions about myself and my skills for the role. At some point, I started to ask Donald about the role and Oracle the business. The questions I'd prepared, which I shared previously, took the majority of the time for the interview. That left the last fifteen minutes of the forty-five minutes for personal questions. After him answering questions and me speaking only when necessary (15 percent of the time) he said:

> **Donald:** Shirley, you seem like you'd be a great fit for us. What would it take for you to join Oracle?
> **Me:** Well, a good offer . . . [*said with a cheeky smile*]
> **Donald (smiling):** Let me talk with management and we'll come back to you. I would like to make you an offer.
> **Me:** Great! When would I be able to see an official offer from Oracle?
> **Donald:** I'll try and get something over to you by the end of the week.
> **Me:** That's perfect as I was hoping to make the decision of where I am going by next week.

Putting a timeline on the offer allows you to keep the conversation going, and it also puts pressure on them to get you what you need and to decide the plan for your future. You'll find that some companies are able to hire quickly and send over offers immediately, while other corporations may take a long time. This is no exaggeration. I was made a verbal offer during my first interview with Oracle. At the time, I'd already become an experienced interviewee due to all the practice I had, which helped build my confidence. Having job offers on the table also gives you more leverage. I ended up with three job offers on the table. All good offers, but my heart again was set on Oracle. I extended the acceptance period on the other offers until I did all the interviews so I could make a final decision.

Note: Some people take the first offer they get. I always advise to get multiple offers and then make a final decision. Maybe you will still take the first offer you received, but at least you know the market and can be confident in your final decision.

Activity: To Summarize on How to Nail the Interview

- Research your interviewer/s.
- Practice your "elbower" questions by writing them out and answering them out loud.
- Create a list of questions to ask during the interview. Remember that an interview is just a conversation, hopefully one that will make you feel more at ease during your next round of interviews!
- Prepare, practice, and practice some more to create the positive, successful conversations you want to have. You got this!

CHAPTER 5

HOW TO NEGOTIATE

#NEGOTIATE 4 YOU

Let us never negotiate out of fear.
But let us never fear to negotiate.
—John F. Kennedy

The following week, I received the official offer from Oracle. My reaction was to literally jump up and down with excitement! The hiring manager, Donald, gave me a call and specifically, I remember telling myself to remain calm and to not be too overly enthusiastic. Donald offered me a starting salary of $44,000 a year, which was low . . . even ten years ago. But I thanked Donald repeatedly and felt so grateful to even be offered a job at Oracle! I swear I literally would have worked for free at the time just to gain experience (luckily, I didn't tell them that) and to have their brand on my CV.

Now that I had the official offer, I sat down and ran though some basic numbers. With an official offer of $44,000 salary, could I actually afford a lifestyle of living and working in San Francisco, California, like I hoped?

✔ Luckily, I had found a four-bedroom apartment in San Francisco with the cheap rent of $1050 a month. The room was small and originally a second living-room, but the cost was right and I had other friends in the apartment.

✔ Utilities were going to be split between my flat mates and me. We had an estimate of utilities from the previous owner, which was $125 a month per person.

✔ From my experience in university, I had a strict budget of $500 a month to buy groceries, which worked for me then, so I assumed I could do the same in San Francisco.

✔ Going out costs and dinners out per month would be $350.

✔ Gym membership: $75 a month.

✔ Public transport ($4.00 a day) = ($4 a day x five days week) = $20 a week x four weeks = $80 a month.

✔ Clothes shopping: $200 a month.

✔ Miscellaneous: $150 a month.

✔ Savings Account: $200 a month.

Opening up Excel, I did some quick math and came to the realization that for basic-living (assuming I stuck to my budget), I would need to bring a total of $2,730 a month in order to get by in San Francisco.

Now I knew my monthly budget for the lifestyle I wanted to live in the Bay Area. But what was the total amount I took home after tax? By using Smart Asset Federal Income Calculator (https://smartasset.com/taxes/income-taxes), I was quickly able to find my take-home amount after tax in the United States. If you are living in

Living Costs:	Monthly Finances ($ Amount)
Rent	$1,050
Utilities	$125
Food (Groceries)	$500
Going out/Dinners out	$350
Gym memebership	$75
Public Transport	$80
Shopping (Clothes)	$200
Other	$150
Savings	$200
Total monthly costs:	$2,730

the United Kingdom, the equivalent would be using the GOV.UK site (https://www.gov.uk/estimate-income-tax), which can help you estimate your income taxes.

With a salary of $44k a year, I would bring a take-home pay of $35,809 a year or $2,984 a month in the United States. In the United Kingdom, if we did the same exercise using the salary number of 44,000 and flipping the currency into GBP for simple math, we would have a take-home of £33,561.80 a year or £2,796.82 a month.

Here is the tax break down for both the United States and United Kingdom:

Tax Type	Marginal Tax Rate	Effective Tax Rate	Taxes
Federal	12%	8.23%	$3,622
FICA	7.65%	7.65%	$3,366
State	6.00%	2.73%	$1,203
Local	0%	0%	$0
Total Income Taxes		18.62%	$8,191
Income After Taxes			$35,809
Retirment Contributions			$0
Take-Home Pay			$35,809

Your estimated take home pay is £33,561.80 a year	
Estimated take-home pay is:	
Income Tax	£6,298.20
National Insurance	£4,140
Total tax to pay	£10,438.20

How we calculate your yearly results:	
Your pay	£44,000
Your tax-free allowance is	£12,509
Your taxable pay is	£31,491

A take-home of $2,984 with a budget of $2,730 a month left me with $254 for miscellaneous spending. This seemed tight to me, especially because I'm not the best with my expenses and finances. From speaking to my peers, I learned quickly that my salary offer was below the norm for San Francisco living (average single household was between $60k and $80k in 2011). It's always good to talk to your peers and get an idea of where you stand in the market when you are going for a job.

Another thing to consider is the benefits offered with the job. Working for Oracle would come with great benefits, some of which were the Employee Stock Purchase Plan (ESPP), which is when employees of a company can purchase the corporation's stock at a discount. You can contribute to the plan through payroll deductions.

They also offered a 401(k) plan as well, which is a retirement savings plan sponsored by an employer. It allows you to save and invest a piece of your paycheck before taxes are taken out. So I could opt into that as well, but if I did that it would reduce my take-home salary, which I needed to get by each month. They also had a great healthcare partner, which is super important to have in the United States.

However, I hadn't included holidays, concert tickets, or traveling in my monthly costs, which were all things I loved and were hoping to do in my adulthood after graduating university. I don't mind working hard, but the whole point of working hard is to have enough left over to have some fun. This was beginning to look like all work and no play.

After reviewing my calculations, I knew I was going to be tight each month. I had two options:

1. take the job as is so I can get the experience
   OR
2. go back and try to negotiate for more money

After I received the offer, my mentor coached me to go back and ask for a higher base salary. Side note: Having a mentor who can help you navigate your first negotiation is really useful; this is someone you can go to when you are unsure or need advice. My mentor suggested that for the initial few months that we meet once a week, to update him on my progress and discuss any obstacles, uncertainties, or questions I had.

Funny enough, even after I did the math and knew it would be tight each month, I still pushed back at my mentor, saying "You know, I just don't feel comfortable asking for more" and "I can't do it." Again, not believing in my position or in myself, thinking that if I went back and asked for more, then they would think I was being selfish and retract the job offer.

Here is a KEY in all aspects of life: It's not what you ask, it's how you ask it.

Negotiating can be uncomfortable, especially if you think your position is weak. An example: You are a recent graduate from college/university and are in the workforce for the first time, or you're changing industries and/or roles altogether, or maybe you're returning to the workforce after an absence or having been off on paternity/maternity leave. All of these things can make you feel unsure or doubtful of whether to ask for more, whatever that more may be. It could be more money or more holidays or more whatever it is you desire. In your head, you feel powerless.

Well, STOP right now.

Everyone, no matter the position, has leverage. They WANT you; so leverage it. They want you because you are a fresh college graduate and they can shape you into their workforce. Or they want you because you've had experience in another industry that they want to know. Or they see something in you that they need. What are you bringing to them? Why are they offering you the job? Ask yourself: what do you have to leverage?

No matter your position or situation, you should ALWAYS negotiate. Asking and negotiating up front can save you a lot of stress and remorse down the line.

Asking for more in the right way can increase your credibility in getting the job. Statistics show that when people negotiate, the other parties respect them more. Showing your negotiation and communication skills during the interview gives the employer an example of how you work with others. It also gives you more insight to see if this really is a place you want to work, establishing whether this company will accommodate your needs. If you decide not to ask and immediately accept the job, then it makes it extremely difficult to turn around in two to four months and ask for something more. Your employer will most likely ask, "Why didn't you ask for this during your hiring process?"

There's always something we want when we go for a job, but how do we go about it in the right way? Early in my career I was introduced to the if-then negotiation tactic, which I continue to use today in my professional and even personal life. "If" I give you what you want, "then" can I have . . . ? You can finish that sentence.

After a few more long talks, I was encouraged by my mentor to go ask for a higher base salary by using if-then statements. For example, "**If** I take the job as is now for $44k a year, assuming I'm hitting all the KPIs (which I will), **then** can we discuss a pay raise six months into my role for $60k where the market average is now?"

I sucked it up and called Donald to see if we could meet the next day to further discuss my offer. He agreed. The next day I remember feeling extremely uncomfortable in his office. Being a twenty-two-year-old negotiating with a manager of a large tech firm with years more experience would make anyone uneasy.

Me: Donald, thank you so much for the offer. I can't emphasize enough how excited I am.
Donald: Good. Well, I hope you accept. What is it you wanted to discuss today?
Me: As much as I appreciate the offer to work here, the offer seems quite low to where the market standards are currently today. The cost of living is quite high in San Francisco and I'm worried $44k while I'm getting up to speed may be too tight. Would it be possible to have a base of $60k, where the market standard is today?
Donald: I can check, but I don't think we'll be able to offer you more.
Me: OK, well, please check with management. I am really excited about the offer, but I need to make sure I

can also get by on my salary until I start making more commission.

Donald: I understand, Shirley; let me see what I can do.

One hour later, Donald called me.

Donald: Hi, Shirley, I checked with management and we would not be able to offer you more base salary. Again, we really hope you take the offer.

Me: OK, understood. Thanks for checking. That's disappointing, but I understand. If I take the job as is now for $44k, assuming I'm hitting all the KPIs (which I will), **then** can we discuss a pay raise six months into my role for $60k base salary? Which is where the market currently is today.

Donald: Hmmm, I think that sounds fair. Why again is $44k too low for you?

Have a reason as to why you are negotiating, whether it's more pay or more paid time off. Why do you deserve more? What's the standard of living in the area? Is your pay at the industry standard? Do you have evidence, and have you calculated your take-home per month? Are other companies in similar fields offering you more? Can you prove it? Bringing it back to the market standard can be very helpful, or bring it back to your personal life. For example, "The reason I am asking for additional holiday is so I can to visit my family in Europe each year and spend time with my aging grandma who raised me."

Me: Well, to be honest—I've done the calculations of my living costs in San Francisco, and after rent I would barely have enough to get by on $44k a year. My rent alone would be almost half of my check per month. So, all I ask is to be considered for a pay raise, once you see what I can do. Does that seem fair to you? Do we have an agreement?

Donald: I agree to review your salary after your first six months and we can discuss it further. No promises, but let's start there.

Me: So, if I accept the offer at $44k, then you will agree to reviewing my salary after six months to where the industry standard is today around $60k?

Donald: Yes, that sounds good.

Note: As you can see from the conversation above, I repeated myself twice to finalize the agreement. Repeating your agreements can solidify the conversation in a person's mind. However, it's even better if you can get that person to confirm in an email.

Me: Donald, would you mind just confirming that in an email? Just so we remember to discuss this again in six months' time? Again, thank you for the offer. I will sign the documents over today, once you confirm our agreement in an email.

Donald confirmed our agreement via email. I then officially accepted and signed the Oracle offer letter the following day with a start date of two weeks later. Six months into my role I met with Donald for a review and, true to his word, I received a pay raise to $60k a year on my base salary.

Unfortunately, I have heard a few stories of people not ask for more during the negotiation period (pre-signing the offer) who decide to ask once they start the job. From personal and secondhand experience, I've found it's more

difficult to negotiate for yourself once you're in the insti-
tution. By negotiating up front, you can go back and say,
"Remember we discussed this up front before I started?
I was very honest and open about my expectations and
what I want. Therefore, when can I see X happen?"

You might ask yourself, well what if they do push
back? Not everyone is a "Donald." Then the question is,
why are they pushing back? Are you asking for something
that is unrealistic? Do you not have a solid proof or reason
as to why you are negotiating? Come armed and ready to
these negotiations. Remind yourself that you are worthy
of what you want in your professional career and you are
the only one fighting for what you want; no one else in the
world will do this for you. And maybe if you can't come
to a fair agreement with them, then the next questions are:
Do you really want to work there, if you can't come to
some agreement on this initial negotiation?

I thought Sheryl Sandberg said it right: "Fake it until
you become it." What would your most authentic and ultimate professional self ask for? Be that person. And start to
become your true professional self.

The key to a successful negotiation is a nonthreatening
conversation. I have seen many individuals make the mistake of threatening the hiring manager when pushing for
a pay raise or salary increase. For example, "If you don't
increase my salary, then I will take the other offer." As you
can see in this sentence, it is all about the individual; there
is no negotiation in this example, *only a threat*. Be careful that your negotiation is not a threat but a trade, where
both sides are getting something positive that they want in
return.

Activity

Practice negotiating in your personal life with your friends and family. Learn how to negotiate in a comfortable setting and work your way up to the workplace.

Good negotiation = both sides walk away happy.

1. Write down what you want in your offer that you currently don't have at the moment. Practice your if-then statements. See if you can start to use them in your personal life, which will help you in your professional life. For example, let's say you and your partner want to go to dinner, but you disagree over which restaurant, which night, which time, and so on. What can you leverage? "If we go to your restaurant tonight for dinner, then will you agree to make dinner for the rest of the week?"

2. Or maybe use it with friends: "If we have drinks at The Ship, then we plan on a movie day Sunday at your place. Deal?"

3. Now try it in a professional setting: "If I work the extra shift next week, then I have the last Friday of the month off. Does that sound fair to you?" Being polite when you negotiate can only help in your negotiation.

Again, play with this skill and see how you can adapt it in your personal life before you try to negotiate in the workplace. What can you leverage? What do you want? Start to play with scenarios and then turn yourself into a negotiation genius with easy if-then trades throughout your daily life!

CHAPTER 6

HOW TO BEHAVE ONCE YOU GET THE JOB—YOUR PERSONAL BRAND

#HOW TO BEHAVE AT WORK

Your personal brand is what people say about you behind your back.

- ✔ I had a signed offer from Oracle.
- ✔ I had negotiated my position.
- ☐ But I was unsure how to behave in the job.
- ☐ I had no brand, yet . . . But, what is a brand?

How you look + How you speak + How you act
= Your Personal Brand

When you start out in your career, it's really important to become aware of how you are perceived in a professional setting. A brand (in terms of working) is creating an image that identifies a person and differentiates them from others at the company. Over time, this image becomes associated with a level of credibility, quality, and satisfaction in the mind of other peers and management. In other words, everyone else kind of decides the content of your brand. Someone once said: a brand is what people say about you behind your back. Think about what type of "brand" you want to have, that is, your reputation at your job. What do you want people to say behind your back?

Let's think through some of the major brands that we have today. Pull up in your mind's eye the logo for Coca-Cola. That red can in white cursive. Or how about McDonald's, with the classic golden arches of the letter M that can be seen from afar. The Nike logo with the swoosh or even Facebook (now Meta) with their classic blue F in a circle.

Let's take Coca-Cola as an example. How does the Coca-Cola brand make you feel? All warm and fuzzy inside? Does it put a smile on your face? The Coca-Cola Company is known for the creation of the red suit for Saint Nicholas (Santa Claus). It's one of the most famous brands in the world. So if you did get the warm fuzzies, it's not by accident.

Let's take another one: Starbucks. It has an image of a green mermaid character, designed to reflect the seductive imagery of the sea. When I see this sign, my mind screams, "Go there! There's coffee!"

Brands make you feel emotion by what they stand for (sell), which is how they have marketed themselves to you. This is very similar to your own brand at work. What emotion will others feel toward you?

One of my first mentors at the company and now a dear friend, Neema, was a hard-working guy, constantly meeting his goals and revenue targets. He was the first to get into the office and the last to leave. My manager looked to him for support and help with the rest of the team. He had been at the company for three years and knew the system well. He had a strong "brand" and was regarded as a go-getter, i.e. ready to jump on any task. When he went up for a promotion, he got it because 1) he'd worked hard, but also because 2) he had a good brand to support him and people felt confident that Neema would get the job done.

Protecting your brand and building on it is very important.

How do you want to be perceived in the office? Are you going to be the hard-worker? The "I'm here to help, let's get the job done" person? Or will you shy away from this and become someone who is not regarded well or not seen as the hardest worker on the floor? Someone who is constantly late for work or doesn't really seem to care? The hungover person on Mondays (because there's always one in the office) or the unhelpful person who says, "I'm not going to do that or help you because it's not my job"?

I remember when I first started at Oracle there was this guy named Ben who joined the team on the same day as me. Ben was straight out of college like myself, and had graduated from an Ivy League school. He had just gone through the six week "Class of" program that our CEO had promoted, which was three hundred college graduates on an intensive six-week training program before being put into the office to sell software.

Like me, this was Ben's first real job out of college. He was nicknamed "The Golden Boy" as he was blond, fit, went to an Ivy League, played lacrosse collegially, and was obviously intelligent. Everyone loved Ben.

Now, it was a Monday morning six weeks into our new job, where we had targets and numbers to hit each week. Monday mornings on a sales floor are the days where your bosses want you to hit the ground running. Show up early and start dialing the phone to call clients. We were expected to make at least fifty calls each day, leading to hopefully a new generation of pipelines and opportunities, which would eventually lead into a sale.

Ben showed up late on this particular Monday morning. He looked disheveled with his tie on loosely, almost as if he had jumped out of bed quickly. He could have gotten away with the look, but it was his voice that gave it away. Ben could barely speak! He had lost his voice, and he was now expected to make sales calls all day on the phone.

Our manager Ken came up to Ben and jokingly asked loudly, "What happened to you this weekend?"

Instead of making up an excuse, Golden Boy Ben said in a croaky voice, "I'm extremely hungover."

Ben had obviously had a big weekend, and instead of calling in sick or working from home, he'd made it into the office. And kudos to him for that! However, this was a mistake. When your boss asks you a question like that, never admit to not giving 100 percent at work. It's treading on thin ice. So be careful. No boss, no matter how cool he or she is, likes to hear that. Better yet, don't be hungover when you have work the next day. I've never been a big Sunday or weekly drinker myself, but I certainly don't recommend it if you want to be taken seriously at work.

This did hurt Ben's brand. At work, you work. You don't let the crazy (party) aspects of your life reframe your work ethic so that it appears you're not giving it 110 percent at work. You need to prove yourself, show your worth, and show others the professional side of you. Everyone is human and we all want to have fun, but there is a time and place for everything. When you are starting out your career and working on your brand, how you want to be perceived in the office is the key to your success going forward.

The lesson from Ben is: don't tarnish your brand by being known as the hungover person on a Monday morning. Being the drunkest at a work event or coming in hungover does not help promote your brand. My recommendation is to stay out of the lime light at work. You don't want to be the talk of the office. Instead, you want to be well thought of and liked.

Think about what that takes in your own environment. Start to think about your brand. What do you want to be known for at your company?

- Coming in early to the office or staying late?
- Pulling colleagues and/or peers aside to ask for extra help and explanations so you can better understand your role?
- Meeting or exceeding the KPIs that have been set out for you?
- Helping other team members succeed? Working closely with management to become successful?
- Listening and following the rules? Asking questions when you are unsure?
- Checking in regularly with your manager to make sure they are happy with your ramp up?

The underlying point is you will need to be relentless in your approach and find a way to be successful. My boss at the company used to say: "'It takes years to build a brand, and only seconds to destroy it."

Don't be the drunken idiot at the Christmas party and/or team social outing and ruin your brand/reputation. Be professional at every event, and keep building your brand to progress the career of your dreams.

Activity: Tips on How to Build a Brand

1. Building a brand at work takes time and effort. When you see an opportunity at work that is relevant, take it, whether it's working an extra project with upper management or trying a new skill that will help you in your future role. Thinking ahead of where you want to be in the future and taking small steps toward that goal through relevant opportunities at work is a great way to start to build on your reputation.

For example, my friend Jon wanted to be a manager. At work there was a management enrollment program for people who were hoping to transition into management. It was a six-week course focusing on the difficulties of managing people. He enrolled in the class, came out as the top student, and was appointed to a management position the following year. As this sounds like a perfect story, there are plenty of ways to slowly move toward your goals. Another great way to build upon your brand is by meeting with people all over the business, especially people who are currently in the role you hope to do in the future. In Jon's example, meeting with other relevant managers in the business to discuss their roles and the challenges also helped build his persona at work, along with building upon his brand.

2. The one that everyone fears: PUBLIC SPEAKING. Now, people can't get to know you or your brand unless you put yourself out there and let them hear what you have to say. This this may seem daunting to many of us, but it's truly something that helps you elevate your brand. Whether that's volunteering to speak at team meetings or to give a pitch at a conference, getting your voice heard is not a bad thing. But make sure to avoid speaking just to

speak—as you want to only speak when you sound intelligent and know what you are speaking about.

When you step onto a stage, whether or not you feel it, other people see you as a leader in an authoritative position. Speaking at events can help others assume you are the leader in your field, again helping to boost your career and build upon your reputation. One may ask: What happens if I fall on my face while public speaking? Won't that hurt my brand?

This is a common fear. Statistics show that most people would rather die than have to public speak. And while that seems like a rather strong reaction, it says something about the resistance to public speaking.

I myself have messed up many times while public speaking, but I always come back and can even say that I now really enjoy public speaking. Like any skill, it takes time and lots of practice to perfect.

> *We are what we repeatedly do. Excellence, then, is not an act, but a habit.*
> —Aristotle, Greek philosopher (384 – 322 BC)

For one of my first big work presentations, I had planned days in advance for it, memorizing my speech and practicing to myself. But then, literally two hours before my presentation, my boss changed my slides. I frantically ran into an open conference room and pored over the new changes. The slides were completely different, from the formatting to the context. I was now profusely sweating. As I walked into the presentation room, there were over sixty colleagues from around the world in the room and I was the youngest by a good eight to ten years. Instead of feeling grateful to be there, I just felt uncomfortable and can even go so far as to say I was terrified. I had never given a speech in a business setting, let alone to my peers.

Walking up to the stage, my legs and hands were shaking. I opened my mouth to start my speech and could not get a word out. I FROZE. Literally no words came out, and I stared at the crowd with a blank expression. Luckily my boss saw that I had frozen and was not in a good state to continue. Or to even start. He ended up taking over. I was then patted on the back and told to sit down.

My colleagues teased me after as the one who "couldn't get her words out." It was embarrassing and quite a dramatic experience for me, as you can imagine. But it gave me something that I didn't have before—the fire in my belly to become a great public speaker, to practice my skill. Many people do not know this about me as I now feel very confident speaking in public. I'd even go so far as to say I love it now! But it took years of going to Toastmasters and other speaking groups to get me to where I am today.

There are many public speaking courses. One of the most famous is Toastmasters International, which is "a US headquartered nonprofit educational organization that operates clubs worldwide for the purpose of promoting communication and public speaking skills."[3] If you do feel the need to practice public speaking this, would be a great place to start. Also, I found it a wonderful place to make new friends and meet other professionals.

Here is the website (https://www.toastmasters.org) where you can look to see the closet Toastmaster group near you! Remember there is nothing embarrassing about improving yourself and admitting you need to work on a

---

3   Wikipedia contributors, "Toastmasters International," *Wikipedia, The Free Encyclopedia,* (accessed June 11, 2022).

skill. I find it quite interesting that it's such a taboo for people to admit that they need help with public speaking. We all need a bit of help with at least some aspects of our skill sets. And everyone—I don't care how many times that they have spoken in public—still gets the butterflies in their stomach when they walk onto that stage. Even famous comedians have shed a light on their fears of public speaking and how they eventually conquered it, falling many times (just like myself) on their face. So, start falling on your face and get practicing!

3. Ask questions at meetings; come prepared with an unusual question or two, which will highlight a concern or topic. Again, don't "speak to speak," but get prepared to add to the discussion. When you say something, you want the others to say "good question" or "I was thinking the same thing!" I've heard the saying, "no question is a bad question" and I think to a degree that it holds true. But also, if you can ask an intelligent, probing question, one that makes other people blink and look at the situation, then that's also good, and maybe a little better than a dumb question. Sometimes, people are too scared to speak up. By preparing your question ahead of time and adding to the conversation, it can only help you build upon your brand.

Asking questions is also a great way to slowly build confidence in your public speaking ability. Again, just like comedians you don't walk onto the stage and do a two-hour set as your first performance. You build upon it by maybe giving one joke, then trying another, then another and so on, until you finally have jokes that take you two hours to deliver. Just like public speaking, start small and grow your confidence through asking the right questions at the right time.

4. Network internally and meet other people/teams. There is no one stopping you from reaching out to other people and grabbing a coffee to understand their roles and teams. It can only help you! When you need something, you can then say or think or share, "Actually I met Sarah in Procurement the other day, maybe she can help us." Networking internally can help you get better perspectives and insights on all the roles and on how the company operates. Reach out to people that you normally do not interact with and ask to go for a cup of tea or coffee with them to discuss their roles. You could even use the interview questions in the earlier chapters to help with your discussion. Remember, people like to help people. So push yourself out of your comfort zone and into new territory. This will help people get to know you around the office and get your brand to be the friendly go-getter in every department!

To summarize: Take relevant opportunities, public speak when you are prepared and know your content, ask questions during meetings, and network internally as much as you can! Build a strong, intentional brand which will help you move up in your career at work.

CHAPTER 7

HOW TO DRESS FOR YOUR JOB

#WHAT TO WEAR TO WORK

Your *STYLE is a strong way of communication.*

If you're planning on being a nurse, doctor, dental hygienist, police officer, firefighter, member of the military, chef, pilot, flight attendant, lifeguard, paramedic, mechanic, or veterinary technician, then you will be required to wear a uniform every day on the job and do not need to think too deeply about your personal style. Understand what the uniform dress code is at your place of employment and follow it.

Unfortunately it's not always that simple. Here are some guidelines to help you figure out the office uniform and make the uniform work for you.

Think about the parts of your body that will show while wearing your uniform.

Do you have tattoos? Piercings? Or do you like to wear large hoop earrings? Chokers? Necklaces? What's allowed at work and what's not? Ask.

My suggestion for style when wearing a uniform is "keep it simple and dress smart." For example, in England people tend to walk into the office wearing three-piece suits. The majority of people wear suits every day. This may seem a little much in other cultures, but it's quite normal in the United Kingdom, especially in London. Traditionally, English culture has always favored very formal attire in the workplace.

In my experience, formal attire gives the perception of professionalism. In the morning when you put on your formal suit (dress, trousers, skirts, etc.) or uniform, you're signaling to the world and to yourself that you are mentally ready to start your job. You should always be "dressing for your next role," whether that's to be a senior person on the team, manager, director, or vice president. Formal attire tells everyone you are ready to be the utmost professional in the workplace. In my opinion, dressing smart has helped me move up in the company and be taken seriously by my more experienced colleagues and customers.

Having said all that, it does depend on the office setting. Nowadays, some companies encourage us to express ourselves through our own personal style in office settings. Make a call on how much you want to express yourself. It can be tricky to get it just right.

Now to get us started, let's start with some basics:

Makeup (for both women and men):
- ✔ Foundation
- ✔ Light eye color (or none at all)
- ✔ Mascara
- ✔ Eyeliner on upper OR lower eyelid (not both) or none at all
- ✔ Blushed or lightly bronzed cheeks
- ✔ Natural or nude lip color. The lipstick should be the only thing that stands out the most. Some of

my favorite colors will be shared later. My Spanish girlfriends usually rock a red lip in the office and it can be very professional.

Earrings: Studs, preferably. Diamond, silver, gold, or pearl studs; long earrings and big hoops are for nighttime and going out on the town.

Tattoos: Cover with a long sleeve undershirt if you can. Some workplaces are very lenient about tattoos. Feel it out in your place of work, but for the initial interview definitely cover up. Around 21 percent of Americans have tattoos.[4] But extreme tattoos on the face or neck can get you fired or restricted to only the back office. Be cautious and really think hard before you go get inked. Is having a neck tattoo or sleeve appropriate at your office? Will this help or hurt your career?

Hair: If long, a ponytail, braid, or down is a sophisticated look—as long as it's clean and washed. Washing your hair and grooming yourself is important. Having hair that looks like you just jumped out of bed does not scream, "I'm ready for this job" and/or "my promotion." Choosing a hair color is very personal. Aim for something that is a natural color. Refrain from pink, blue, orange, purple, and other bright hair colors. Invest in dry shampoo that saves you from having to wash your hair in the shower multiple days in a row, and which can give you a fresh hair look when you need it.

---

4   History of Tattoos. "Tattoo Statistics—How Many People Have Tattoos?" June 2022.

Personal hygiene: Some people are unaware of their body odor and smell. Being in the office or a small space with others, you tend to notice smells (good and bad). Using body wash or soap to clean your skin, along with deodorant every day, is a good way to keep your odors to yourself. Find a way to keep your teeth clean (brush daily—once in the morning and once in the evening): some people bring toothbrushes to the office! Be aware of your odors and stay on the safe side of not being the "smelly" person in the office.

Perfume: It's not a good idea, if only because some people are allergic. So save it for nighttime and parties.

Nail color shades:
- ✔ Red, white, and nude are reasonable and preferable in an office setting
- ☐ Shades of green, blue, orange, black, purple, yellow—although fun, these can come off as childish in a professional environment. To be clear: When it comes to appearance, I'm definitely not saying don't be an individual and don't be different than everyone else. By all means, you should be different and unique in your own way. But when it comes to appearance in the workplace—less is more. Coming into an interview with bright purple hair, big hoop earrings, and tattoos all over your arms is completely fine, but will likely not land you the job, as statistics show people like people who are similar to them. Depending on the hiring manager, tattoos, piercings, and brightly colored hair may discourage them from hiring you.

My friend's sister, who lives in Sydney, Australia, has tattoos all over her body. The only part of her body with no ink is her face. She has neck, hand, foot, stomach, back, and full arm sleeve tattoos. Upon trying to get a job she had a very difficult time, even though she was perfectly qualified and had experience in the role. Management wanted her to fully cover her neck tattoos during working hours. In Australia, when it's 30°+ Celsius (85°+ Fahrenheit) in summer, wearing a turtleneck is not very realistic or comfortable. She ended up taking a job she was overly qualified for and with less pay.

How can you make sure your personal style is not compromised and your style does not comprise your potential job? I'm not a stylist myself, but I do have my own personal style that makes me feel good when I walk into the office. I feel confident when I give a presentation because I dress smart, which is half the battle. Before you even open your mouth, people judge you on your appearance. So, make it easy and find a style that suits you professionally.

Office style is tedious and can be very time-consuming for both women and men. Many offices have a dress code, which you should try to understand during your interview process. Women have an abundance of clothing choices, from pants to dresses to suits to skirts, and men also have many choices from trousers to khakis, collared shirts to tweed jackets.

Here are some questions to keep in mind as you progress through your job interview:

- What seems to be the appropriate dress code in the job? What's allowed and what's not?
- What is the vibe in the office? More casual or formal? Are some people wearing jeans?

- Is it a start-up? If so, many start-ups are pretty casual, so coming in a full suit (jacket and trousers) would scream "not the right fit" culturally. However, many companies still expect employees to wear a suit daily, so understanding the culture and the style expectations in the specific office/job is good to discover in your interviews.
- Is there a "casual dress Friday" or "dress down Friday"? If so, this adds a complicating factor. You have to figure out the rule-bound dress code for Monday through Thursday, and then a looser guide for Friday.

Rule of thumb: If you have to question it, then don't wear it. Low-cut shirts, high-riding skirts, shorts, sandals (flip-flops), and stiletto heels are most likely on the forbidden list in your office. Edge on the side of caution with your outfit choices for work, especially in the beginning.

Finding a style that suits your body type is important for your confidence. When you feel good and think you look good, then you tend to also perform well.

There's an old saying: Dress for the job you want—not the one you have. Again, by appearing to be professional and dressing smart, this actually portrays to others (and yourself) that you are ready to be taken seriously and professionally in your career.

What to Wear in the Interview 101: WOMEN—Wear a Suit!

Women should wear a suit (skirt and trousers with a jacket, dress and skirt with a jacket, and/or trousers and skirt with a jacket). Sometimes you can combine colors and styles; for example, wear black trousers with a white and black stripped jacket. Have a nice blouse or shirt underneath your jacket, in case you would like to take it off during the interview. Again, when you walk into that interview room, meeting the interviewer for the first time, look your absolute best.

For example, a black jacket with matching pants or skirt is very acceptable. Work styles tend to come in black, royal blue, gray, or navy. Matching this with a natural colored blouse or white/black shirt will give you a professional style and communicate you are here for your interview.

Key things to avoid in your clothing choices are outfits that show cleavage. So look for tops that end close to the neckline. Additionally, look for skirts that are long— just above the knee or between the ankle and knee. Heels are optional depending on your preference. Ideally, shoes should be easy to walk in and can be worn all day as you will typically be moving around to and from the job interview. Some suggestions:

- Low heels (one to two inches).
- Wedge heels are comfortable and also look smart in the office.
- Flats can be super comfortable while also providing a professional look, along with flat scandals for the summer.
- Sneakers have now become a trend in office style.

Shoes to avoid:

- Shoes difficult to walk in, like four- to five-inch heels, are not very professional. These shoes can be classified as sexy, which is not office appropriate.

- Avoid patent heels, as these tend to be frowned upon in an office setting. Patent heels tend to be for parties or nights out.
- Any ankle-tying shoes with a high heel. Although fun, these should be worn outside the office.
- Flip-flops tend to be a no-no in office settings.

Women can tend to be a bit more creative with outfits compared to men, as women have a wider range of choices. For example, with skirts there are many different styles you could wear to the office: pencil skirt, wide flowy skirt down to the ankle, button skirt that has a length between the knee and ankle, and any fitting skirt just above the knee.

Finding a style that suits you is key to helping you feel more comfortable and hopefully confident in the office. Women even have a huge range of different trouser styles, for example ankle trousers that end just around the ankle. These trousers are best paired with flat shoes. There are wide leg trousers that go to the top of your foot and can be paired with a slight heel. And skinny fit trousers that are tight fitting down to the ankle are great paired with a low heel sandal for the summer or flat for the winter.

Again, the list can go on with our choices. Figure out which style makes your body type look and feel good. Many people find it challenging to find clothes that help bring out their physical features.

There are many different body types. Next are four typical main categories that most women fit in. I have suggestions of what style typical works with each body type; again, it's a suggestion rather than a fact. You will have to decide for yourself what looks best on you!

WOMEN'S BODY SHAPES

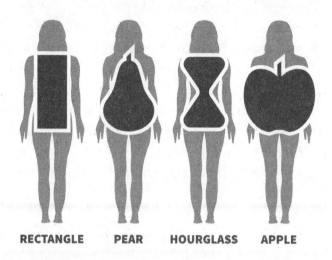

RECTANGLE   PEAR   HOURGLASS   APPLE

Rectangle shaped: meaning long, slim upper body, waist, and lower body—a.k.a. a stick. Pencil skirts are a must! They emphasize your slim figure, giving you a shape, while still appearing professional. With the pencil skirt, you can put on a loose top that flares out on bottom or tuck into your skirt to give you more of a figure. Also, scoop-neck and sweetheart tops with high-waisted trousers and fit-and-flare dresses can be nice styles for rectangle-shaped women.

Pear shaped: meaning curvy hips, thick thighs, and full rear. Choose bright tops that draw attention to the torso and away from the hips. Find dresses that extend the torso and draw attention to it. Examples of good pear styles would be: A-line and wrap dresses, along with square and cowl neck tops and bootcut trousers.

Hourglass shaped: meaning your hips and bust are almost equal in size and you have a clear defined waist that's narrower than both. You want to accentuate the waist by wearing high pants/skirts with a loose shirt tucked in. You can use belts with dresses to bring attention to your waist. Since an hourglass figure is slimmest at the waist, you want to bring attention to your curves. Avoid baggy clothes or too tight clothes that may make you look like you're drowning in fabric or bring attention to areas where you carry more weight. Think: belted jackets, fitted tops with a wrap close to the waist, skinny and flared trousers that bring the attention back to your waist.

Apple shaped: meaning slim lower body and carrying weight around your waist. Look for skirts with a waistband that would hit at the smallest part of your torso and flare over the stomach. For dresses, you can do ones that have a waistband just under your lungs and below the knee. In addition, Empire waist dresses, V-neck and wrap tops, and straight or slim trousers are a great style for apple-shaped women.

There are so many different body types that it would be hard to list them all. And of course most of us fall somewhere in between. It's a rare person who is completely one type or another. Hopefully I've given you an idea about your appearance and how it is important to not only feel good (most important), but also how to look good in your choice of work clothes, especially for the interview. My recommendation would be to go online and search for work styles under your body type. I found the Nordstrom "Dressing for your Body Type: A Guide" very useful in the past (www.trunkclub.com/womens-style/female-body-shapes).

What to Wear in the Interview 101: MEN—Wear a Suit!

Men should wear a matching suit (trousers, collared shirt, and jacket with a tie). Now, some men might cringe when I suggest wearing a tie, but again you want to be your best-dressed self! Whereas women can get away with combining different suit colors and styles, men should stick to matching suits, especially for the interview. One thing that varies in countries is the fit and style of a suit. In America, men tend to wear suits that are loose and not very fitted; in Europe men go the opposite way and wear very fitted suits. Find a suit that fits your body type and makes you feel good. Some good examples are black or navy suits with a white-collar shirt and a colorful tie. The tie can match the suit or, if it's a black suit, you can play with the colors (purple, blue, etc.).

For men I would suggest getting two different suits colors, for example, black and blue. That way you can wear a different color and change suits if you are doing multiple interviews with the same company. If you only have one suit, then change your collar shirt and tie for the next interviews. Depending on your budget, it might make sense to have one nice suit and then multiple collar shirts.

In general, office wear tends to vary depending on the company culture. I know for some people in banking, for example, they wear a suit every single day to the office, which is expected attire for every employee. In comparison, in the technology industry trousers and a collar shirt is appropriate, even jeans if he or she (the employee) is not seeing their customers on that given day. Some people pair black jeans or dark jeans with collared shirts. Always edge on the side of caution. When you think of your style, remember to dress to impress. So look smart, but not too overdressed.

Matching your belt and shoes is a nice touch and tends to help with the dressing smart approach. Many shoe places will sell matching belts with their shoes or you can buy the shoes and go find a matching belt. Also, socks are something that are also required with a suit. Typically, the classic look is for socks to be long and black. Some men like to wear colorful socks that show when you are sitting down. These seem to add flavor to a suit, while also appearing to be trendy.

Remember to wear a belt as, otherwise, it looks almost like you are half-dressed! Nowadays, many men wear trousers with a collar shirt and no jacket. This is a nice work style as well and is not too dressy for a day in the office.

Putting a cardigan over a collar shirt with a nice pair of shoes and jeans also looks classy and smart. This would be a great outfit for a Friday in the office or maybe for an interview at a start-up, depending on the vibe in the office.

Here is an easy chart to match your suit color with your shoes. I would take note of this when shopping for new outfits. Try to find shoes, suits, and collar shirts that can mix and match to allow you more variety of outfits. Based on the chart, my advice would be to go for the classic black shoes, which tend to go with the majority of suit colors.

Matching Suits & Shoes			
Suit Color	Black Shoes	Light Brown Shoes	Dark Brown Shoes
Black Suits	YES	NO	NO
Charcoal Suits	YES	NO	NO
Navy Suits	YES	NO	YES
Grey Suits	YES	YES	NO
Light Grey	YES	YES	YES

Again, it's more of a rule of thumb than anything else. Even though you may buy a nice suit, typically you will still need to take it to a tailor to fit to your body type. Make sure to choose the fit that is right for you that is not too tight and not to baggy. In general, most dry cleaners will have a tailor or would know where you could find one.

ACTIVITY

It's time to get your work wardrobe together and up-to-date! Here are a few questions we need to start to think about:

1. What is your body type? What outfits are appropriate for your body type?
2. Do you have work-appropriate clothing or do you need to go to the store and update your wardrobe? Below are some affordable stores to consider:

US:
- Amazon ($)
- H&M ($)
- T.J. Maxx/Marshalls/Ross ($)
- Target ($)
- ASOS ($)
- Consignment/Secondhand shops ($)—you can find some hidden gems! If you're on a very tight budget, take a look at your local consignment/charity shop. You may be surprised at the beautiful professional outfits people give away and you can buy for cheap. Personally, I purchase a lot of my favorite work outfits from these shops.
- Macy's ($$)

- Nordstrom Rack ($$)—Outlets still have the great brands, but will be cheaper. See if you can find one around your area!

UK:

- Zara ($)
- ASOS ($), online retailer
- M&S ($)
- Consignment/Charity shops ($)—you can find some hidden gems! If you're on a very tight budget, take a look at your local consignment/charity shop. You may be surprised at the beautiful professional outfits people give away and you can buy for cheap. Personally, I purchase a lot of my favorite work outfits from these shops.
- Massimo Dutti ($$)
- Reiss ($$$)

3. How many outfits do you have? Can we mix and match suits? If you only have one or two suits, how many shirts do you have that we can bring into the mix? What type of shoes, belts, or accessories can you use to make it look like a different outfit?

4. The most important thing is to find outfits that you love and help you feel good as you walk into your job. Do you feel good and look good? Do your clothes portray the brand and vision you have for your future desired self?

CHAPTER 8

HOW TO REACH YOUR CAREER AMBITIONS

#CAREER AMBITIONS

Now returning to my career goals, you might be thinking, "Well done, Shirley. You work at Oracle. You got what you wanted!" And I was pretty happy. I mean, I was over-the-moon happy. However, life is never that simple. Working at Oracle met the majority of my career aspirations, but not all.

- ✔ I had started to build my brand.
- ✔ I was dressing appropriately for the job I wanted, not the one I had.
- ✔ I was working in an international company.
- ☐ I wasn't yet doing multi-million-dollar deals.
- ☐ I wasn't yet working abroad.

After a full year of working the phones as an inside sales representative in Redwood Shores for Oracle, I was finding myself scraping by on small deals and not the mega-millions I had envisioned. It was hard work, despite these being only small deals (around $50k), and the hours were heartbreaking. Most days I found myself close to tears on my hour-long commute back home.

One day while speaking to a friend, I learned about the Oracle recruitment application, where employees can view every available job around the world posted by the company, as well as each position's hiring manager. I logged in the next day and came across my dream job. It was for a field role, which would mean no more cold-calling but instead meeting customers in person. The job location was in the United Kingdom—a job abroad! My dream had always been to travel back over the pond and live in Europe. To think I could potentially move up in the organization, get a promotion to be a field representative, and LIVE IN LONDON: "Sign me up!"

I immediately contacted the hiring manager in London asking whether or not he was still accepting applicants and crossed my fingers as I wrote the email.

About an hour later, it became apparent that this poor British gentleman was awfully confused as to why someone from California was emailing him about a job. He replied cc-ing a colleague with the same name as his in the United States, convinced that I'd made some kind of mistake. I was just about reply to confirm that I indeed wanted to apply for the role, when I received a second email a mere five minutes later saying that if I hadn't made a mistake and was interested in the role, then he would be happy to speak with me!

I was ecstatic. We planned to speak on Skype about a week later.

Phil, the hiring manager: Top of the morning to you, Shirley. Lovely to meet you.

Me: Hi, Phil, thanks for speaking with me.

Phil: No problem. So, tell me, why are you interested in a job in England?

Me: Well, Phil, I attended university in Barcelona and fell in love with Europe. Since I graduated from college—five years ago now—my goal has always been to return to the European continent and eventually to work abroad for my company. I've had great successes over the past year and a half, and I'm now looking for my next career move. Are you still looking to fill the position on your team?

Phil: Yes, I am actively looking for someone. Tell me about this success you've had over the last year.

It was overall a very positive call. I enquired about the team and his experience and learned that Phil was a new manager looking to expand his relatively young team. He wanted people that were hungry and willing to work hard. He had never hired someone from outside of the United Kingdom before, but knew people who had and was willing to take a chance on the right candidate.

He told me that he thought I could be a good fit and the next stage would be to talk to his boss, the VP, Jack O'Connell, whom I came to understand was a BIG name. Jack ran one of the bigger organizations in the United Kingdom with fifty salespeople. The next step would be to present a business plan to Jack over Skype, detailing my vision for running the territory.

I had passed stage one. Woo-hoo!

Without even thinking, I immediately did what none of us are supposed to do, but often find ourselves doing anyway: I started to prepare for the presentation by creating a twenty-page slide deck outlining "Why Shirley?" We aren't supposed to do this is because we are spending our precious time focusing on the task that may never happen. Instead we should be looking and thinking about the big picture, and asking ourselves the tough questions: Who will be my audience? What would they want to see?

Four days before my big interview, I was continuing to update and perfect my slides. I showed my mentor the presentation. He said, "This is great, but you're missing one huge thing. You need to figure out who you're dealing with. You have no inside information on this Jack. Can you call someone that knows him and get some background on the guy? You have no idea if he's a straight-shooter or likes to be fluffed up. The presentation only works if you know your audience."

I didn't know my audience (AGAIN). The first time I interviewed with Oracle, I was able to use my connection with Michael and find out some inside scoop on the managers, but now I was on my own. But then I remembered that five months prior to this I had actually worked on an international Oracle deal during which I'd teamed up with a British representative. He didn't work for Jack, but he did work in the United Kingdom and, after a quick look at both of their LinkedIn profiles and Oracle's internal information portal, they even appeared to work in the same office building.

I decided to call the guy I had spoken to once about a random deal months ago. His name was Ben, and by some crazy stroke of luck that day, he picked up.

Ben: Hello, this is Ben. How can I help?
Me: Hi, Ben, this is Shirley at Oracle in California. You may not remember, but we worked on a deal about five months ago. Would you have a few minutes for me?

Ben: Sure, what is this about?

Me: Well, funnily enough, I have been interviewing for a position at Oracle in the UK, and I have an interview in four days with one of your VPs, Jack O'Connell. I was wondering whether you knew him and could perhaps give me some advice, or information about him.

Ben (laughs): Shirley, too funny! Yes, I know him well. I'm actually on holiday today, but may I call you back tomorrow to discuss?

Me: Yes, of course. Thanks, Ben! I'd really appreciate that. I'll find some time in your calendar and throw in an invite.

Ben made time for a thirty-minute call with me the following day. He not only knew Jack, my interviewer, but better yet, he knew what type of person and leader he was:

- He was a no-bullshit kind of guy—a straight-shooter.
- He was Irish and liked a few drinks.
- He had developed his career in Oracle, and liked to promote people within the organization.

Could Ben also give me some personal information about Jack? Heck yes! He told me Jack's favorite football team was Liverpool, and he was really hoping they'd win the FA Cup.

So, what was the FA cup? Where was Liverpool . . . ? In all honesty, I had no idea. But my new friend Ben made it very clear to me that if I was somehow able to mention Liverpool Football Club and them winning the FA cup, I would, in his words, "get the job, mate!" We laughed and I thanked him for his time and help. Boy, the English are a lovely bunch!

Interview day came around and the Skype call had been scheduled for 2 p.m. UK time, which is 5 a.m. California time. I was nervous but prepared. I knew my stuff, I had insight into the interviewer which I guessed he wouldn't be expecting, and I even knew his favorite football team.

The interview kicked off fine. We covered the basics, my path, my success history, my current situation, why I wanted to move, etc. And then we came to the famous, "Why should I hire you?" question. I made it clear that I was the best candidate because I do my research, I know my customers, and I get to know my audience. And the kicker, "I, too, Jack, want Liverpool to win the FA Cup."

Jack stopped and stared at me.

"You're hired," came out his mouth, along with a huge smile and a few claps. Another hiring manager named Matt was in the room with Jack and looked really shocked. Matt stared back at me as if to say, *How the hell did you know that? You're all the way out in California!*

I smiled, and thanked them for their time. Three days later I got a call confirming that I'd officially landed my dream job in the United Kingdom working a multi-million-dollar territory for Oracle. I was over the moon.

Within my first week in London, Matt approached me and said, "I have to ask, how did you know that Jack's favorite team was Liverpool? I still can't figure it out."

I smiled, and said, "Research."

In summary, when you go for your dream role, leave nothing to chance. Get the job because you were highly prepared and knew your audience. Plan to negotiate before you sign the contract, and always keep your brand in mind—make sure you're being perceived exactly how you want to be.

Another piece of advice is to utilize your company for your own career gains. I remember a female colleague once advising me, "Use the company to your advantage, Shirley. Take everything you can from your company to improve yourself, your career, and your life. Be selfish." At the time, I felt quite uncomfortable with the thought. I was only in my first job at that point, and I felt obligated to the company, almost as if I really owed them for hiring me.

Now with the benefit of hindsight, I entirely agree with my colleague. So many companies offer classes or pay for supplementary courses in the hope of retaining their employees. There are benefits at every company of which employees should take full advantage. Use the system for your own "selfish" needs to reach your career goals and even to pursue personal passions, non-work-related passions, or whatever makes you feel good.

Now, I'm not suggesting that you should take a company card and go buy your significant other a fancy dinner. But use perks to your advantage because it also benefits the business. For example, when I moved to London, a friend of mine sent me a list of the best restaurants in town categorized by neighborhoods. It took her two years to compile. One of the great benefits of working in sales is attending luncheons and dinners with my customers, so I used this opportunity to work my way down the list and "taste" my way through the city. And actually, the customers loved it because very often they hadn't been to whatever restaurant I'd chosen—so it was a fun experience for all. And the best part is my company fronted the bill!

So, check out what's on offer at your choice of work and make sure to reap the rewards.

ACTIVITY

What opportunities at your company can you exploit to help you achieve your long-term goals? Courses? Management seminars? Or perhaps simply extending a work trip over a weekend to enjoy seeing more of the world? Be bold, be true to your company, and get what you want out of your career and your life.

Plan for your career. Make a six-month, a one-year, and a three-year plan. These plans don't need to be set in stone. Obviously, situations can change and you may even change your mind about your career, but planning your career aspirations allows you to check yourself. Ask yourself: Am I on the path to my life goals? Why do I want them? What do I need to do to achieve these aspirations? Have my aspirations changed? Where will I be in six months, one year, and three years?

There is something powerful about writing things down. About telling yourself and the world *I am going to make this happen.* I want to give you a little example. At the time of writing—in my local Thai Noodle Bar in Chelsea, London, to be precise—I currently have three goals:

1. Publish my book.
2. Reach a wider audience of readers and sell over a million copies.
3. Inspire young professionals through talks (virtual and in-person) around the world with my book and help them reach their career aspirations.

These are my career aspirations. Our fears and self-doubts are our only limitations. Remember we can get anything we want in life—we just need to believe in ourselves and then make it happen. But when we put them down we also run the risk of including pie-in-the-sky goals that are ludicrous or contradictory. I have a friend whose life's ambition is to be on the bridge of the starship *Enterprise,* exploring strange new worlds and new civilizations, boldly going where no one has gone before. And I want to say good for her, *You go!* But Starfleet Academy has not yet been founded. So it's good to have a reality check. To help with that, let's put a different lens on this activity:

1. What can't you bear to do? What always falls off your to-do list? Even though you're broke, what task is so awful that you're willing to hire someone to do it? That reality is something you need to organize around and might influence your ability to achieve your ambitions. For my friend who loves *Star Trek,* she couldn't bear to do sciences.

2. What's your worst-case scenario? Can live with it? For my friend, her worst-case scenario was spending her time watching TV, reading sci-fi, and attending Comic Con. She can live with that.

3. What's your Plan B? How reasonable is that Plan B? For my friend, Plan B is to work abroad in exotic locations that are strange and kind of dangerous.

4. What's your escape hatch and consolation prize? If Plan B fails, and so does Plan C, what do you do? The answer you give is your escape hatch. What you still have that makes you say to yourself, "At least I still have this": that's your consolation prize.

5. What's driving you? That's so deeply personal you reasonably might not even know. It requires

self-awareness, and even the best of us struggle with that one. Plus what drives us changes as we grow. So this one is tough to answer. But if you do that, then the other four tasks in this activity become clearer.

CHAPTER 9

HOW TO HANDLE RELATIONSHIPS AND POLITICS ON THE JOB

#POLITICS AT WORK

Have you ever watched a television show or film that highlights the politics of doing the job? They're usually full of drama, scandals, and love affairs. As we know, most shows and film are meant to be for entertainment, but can have some real-life elements to them. Why do we work? Have a career? What drives each and every one of us?

We all have different reasons.

And those different reasons can have an impact on you. For some people, it's money, recognition, or power that drives them and their actions in the office. Other people just want to do their job and get home to their family. Some people are working to get themselves through school; others are working to pay off debts or loans. We all have a driver. I hope by now you'll know what type of person you are and what's driving you.

When you start your new job/career, it's good to be conscious of the politics that swirl beneath the surface of the job. Try to recognize what drives certain individuals and understand the driver for each person you work with. For example, Ed has two kids and wants to buy a new house with more space in his town. He is the primary breadwinner and needs to make more in order to get a bigger mortgage. He is a prime example of someone who desires more money and is driven to earn more. In comparison, Lucy is a young professional who has always seen herself in a leadership role; she is living at home still, but wants to build her own team. Lucy is more driven by recognition. Neither is bad or good, but each driver gives you an idea of where that individual is coming from.

Remember that people's actions are based off of their thoughts and emotions. If you can understand or get an idea of their thoughts or where they want to go or what they want to do, then you are one step closer to deciphering their actions and, ultimately, the politics at work.

Political gain is seeking to make political capital out of situations with the main aim being to gain more influence, money, prestige, or support. Some people are natural politicians and it can be difficult to truly see what's going on or deal with it, while others find themselves being forced into politics in the workplace. My recommendation is having your eyes open to the political situations in your office and to be conscious of their existence, which can help you prepare for your own future. Politics exist. They can be uncomfortable. Regardless of whether you have two people or two thousand in your office, there will be politics on the job.

Building your brand properly is the best way to gain political recognition. Taking the time to understand the individuals in your office, their drivers, and the political game helps you prepare for your own advancement. You cannot get ahead if you don't understand the landscape and where to go next to reach your destination.

And look, you don't have to be Sigmund Freud, figuring out people's hidden psyche so that you can achieve
at the job. First, if that's how you're spending your time,
you're not going to have a lot of time left over to actually
do your own job. Second, I'm not sure Freud was able to
figure it out either. Third, it can be kind of obvious.

Let me give you an example.

In a former job, we had a vice president, Bill, who was
quite influential and powerful. He was driven purely by
retaining power in his organization. He was a tyrant and
liked to show everyone that he was the boss and the person in charge; one might even go so far as to call him a
"diminisher." From my perspective, Liz Wiseman said it
best in her study of leadership, *Multipliers*. There are two
types of leaders in the world:

> **Diminisher** = Leader who does not leave room for oth-
> ers to think freely, tells other people what to do, and
> always needs to be the smartest person in the room.
> **Multiplier** = Leader who uses their intelligence to
> amplify the smarts and capabilities of people around
> them.[5]

Bill liked to bring good people into his organization and
basically just tell them what to do and drain their intelligence and energy. He made a little crew around him at
work that he protected and continued to manage indirectly. We called his crew "Billie-idiots," as they kissed
the ground he walked on, always doing activities together
outside of work, and were very proud of the fact that they

---

5   Liz Wiseman, *Multiplers: How the Best Leaders Make Everyone
     Smarter* (New York: Harper Business, 2017).

were in this tight-knit crew for their own political gain. When it was promotion time, guess who went up the ladder? The Billie-idiots, even though they were not the top performers.

Unfortunately for these individuals, our corporation finally caught on to Bill and his crew. My guess is many people complained to Human Resources that there was unfair treatment going on, and Bill was eventually fired. The Billie-idiots were left and then had a big issue. They'd never tried that hard when Bill was around as he protected them in the workplace. Now, they were being scrutinized; several were let go and forced to leave the business.

Be careful with whom you decide to associate and team up with at work. Follow your own heart and values in the workplace. Don't let others' opinions sway your judgment at work. Remember that you are the best judge of how you should conform in the workplace. Don't let your own personal code fall apart in order to advance. Being friends with people at work makes your job enjoyable. We're all human beings who rely on connections, human touch, acknowledgment from others, and love. So connecting with people at work is super powerful for your professional gain and hopefully also your personal well-being. Nonetheless, be cautious of who you decide to befriend and make sure their values are aligned with your own.

Finding a mentor at work will help you gain confidence and network within the company. They can also give you advice on the political side of work. Take time to understand the politics at play and understand the game you have entered. One of the things I always do when starting a new job is to find the best person in my department— that is, the person who everyone else goes to for help or guidance. There's always someone on the team who stands above the rest. Finding a peer who can also be a champion for you within the organization will help you ease into your own role and allow you to talk through your "unknowns."

Here are some questions to ask your mentor/champion/ trustworthy person on the team:

- Who is the big dog at work? Anyone I need to watch out for? Can you talk me through the politics as you see it?
- If I want to achieve X in three years' time, what are the steps I should take? Whose approval do I need to seek? Best upper management to network with?
- Things newbies should know? Do/not do?
- Anything you wish you had done sooner when starting out in the company?
- What are the values of the company that I must follow?
- Can I come to you with questions in the future? I'm sure I will have more.

You can see this as something dirty and political. Or you can see it as a reasonable thing that everyone should do who wants to be a useful employee and do the job as best as is possible. This isn't an invasion of privacy or a second-guessing of someone. It's instead keeping your eyes and ears open so that you dodge the ugliness, step around the problems, and sideline the trouble before it hits you.

Also keep in mind something: what goes around comes around. If someone is playing politics at the office and it's affecting others, then chances are that sooner or later, it'll end in tears.

Politics is a funny game. People spend years trying to rise to the top, and sometimes it can take just a day to destroy them. There are many people who rise to the top by bullying others. I find this approach old-fashioned and I've seen it bite people in the long run. There is no reason why we can't be kind to others. If people bully, it's usually because they have low self-esteem and are doubtful of their own competency.

I had this one senior vice president (SVP) who was notorious for bullying people. People working for this SVP would be shaking with fear before entering his room. This particular SVP had a big role at the company—he was managing a large territory for the sales leaders worth over $150 million of turnover a year. He had a hundred people reporting to him, and his direct reports were all managers who had their own teams of eight to ten people. He was known for being rude and mean and for bullying people to make them feel small and unimportant. There were two options if you worked with him: 1) he either liked you and you got by with only one or two rude comments directed at you while in his presence; or 2) the opposite—he did not like you and you got bullied constantly. This would come in forms of yelling at you for your incompetence or asking over and over again why you were even given your position if you (and I quote) "can't figure it out by yourself" or "why try—you're an idiot."

How someone who bullies people even gets into a position of power is something I still can't wrap my head around. But in corporations, all types of people slip through the cracks and find ways to the top.

At the time, this particular company was going through a rough patch. I had personally thrown in my hat and taken a role outside the firm, but still had friends on the inside. This SVP started to have the tide go against him. The company was changing and new people were coming in at a higher level and bringing in their A-teams. All of a sudden, this SVP was fired for no apparent reason other than that the executives had decided to let him go.

Oh, how the mighty fall.

And to be wholly honest: oh, how I enjoyed watching the mighty fall.

Here was this SVP—top of his game a few months ago—now without a job. Not to mention, he had two high school age kids and a partner who was not working. He now had to go out and find a new job.

During this time, I got a ping from a hiring manager and a recruiter about a potential candidate. It was the infamous SVP from my former company wanting a job at my current place of work. I was asked point-blank if we should hire him. My response was honest: "Unless you want a bully at work, do NOT hire him." And they didn't. From my experience, it seems the higher up you go in an organization, the easier it is to fall and fall fast.

Moral of the story: remember that your legacy (good or bad) follows you wherever you go. People below you can help or hurt you getting a future position. Be kind and know that those who are not kind likely have it coming to them in the future.

ACTIVITY
Take note of which leaders you admire in your company and which leaders you don't.

- What characteristics do the leaders have that you admire?
- Are they leading by example or by fear?
- Which leader do you admire the most? If you are without a job, think about the leaders around the

world you do know; they can be philanthropists or politicians. What do you like about them? What type of approach do they have that inspires you to act or change or do something?

- What can you change about your own way of interacting with others so that your behavior mirrors those whom you admire?

CHAPTER 10

HOW TO BE RESILIENT AND LEARN FROM FAILURE

#LEARN FROM FAILING HARD

No one—NO ONE—gets anywhere by just constantly achieving and winning. Failing, and failing hard, is part of the journey to achieving your goals. I find it funny how we speak constantly about our achievements and praise each other for our success. I think it would be much more beneficial to praise our failures and push each other to try again. Failing should be seen as part of the adventure to your desired destination.

> *Failure should be our teacher, NOT our undertaker.*
> *Failure is delay, NOT defeat. It is a temporary*
> *detour, NOT a dead end.*
> —Denis Waitley

A few years ago, I hit my first real hurdle in my career. I was tired of the corporate world, feeling like I was not really being challenged and like I needed a fresh start. This led me to start interviewing at start-ups around the world. At the time, I thought I had found a light through my boredom and exhaustion of my current circumstance via a chance encounter at the gym. Changing in the locker room in my local London gym, I met a woman who was moving to New York City. Gabby was moving with her AI company. I laughed and said, "I'm currently interviewing at an AI start-up back in San Francisco!" She asked me what I did, and I told her I was a salesperson. She informed me that her boss was looking for a salesperson to join the team in the London branch and recommended that I have a conversation with him.

Life has a funny way of putting people together. You never know where you will get your next job. Could be in the locker-room at the gym, on a plane, at a golf club, or even on vacation! Funnily enough, when you're all prepared to do one thing, life then throws you a curveball. I wasn't ready to move home to California, but didn't see many options as I was tied to a visa in the United Kingdom with my current company. So my options were to move home and find a new job, or find another company to sponsor me in the United Kingdom.

My new friend Gabby asked for my contact details and followed up with me a day later where she introduced me to her boss, James. James invited me to breakfast to discuss a potential job offer. He asked that I meet with him at the Arts Club, which is a very posh private social club in London. It was my first time being invited to the Arts Club and I wasn't quite sure what to expect, but as I walked into the club with high elaborate ceilings, fancy white tablecloths, and large velvet chairs, I was immediately impressed. From the corner I spotted a lanky, slim, and quite tall Englishman with round glasses staring at me as I entered and starting to wave in my direction. Assuming this was James, I started to walk over to his table. James was wearing a green tweed suit with a fashionable thin tie. He jumped up to shake my hand with a huge smile. He spoke at a slow pace and said, "Pleasure to meet you. Thanks for meeting me" in the poshest English accent I'd ever heard.

James and I took a few moments to make acquaintances by discussing where we lived in London and our backgrounds, and learned quickly that we were both one of four children. James was kind and he put me at ease, even though these luxurious surroundings weren't my typical norm.

We discussed the AI company, which was in a niche market. The team was growing and they needed experienced salespeople. After twenty minutes of questions and answers, I was starting to get the feeling that this start-up had huge potential. The people seemed incredible as they were from all over the world with the headquarters in Pakistan; it was a very international company. From my conversation with James, I understood that the sales boss had flown about half the company out for his wedding in Jamaica the year before, so the company culture seemed like a tight-knit group. The technology was very interesting, as well; they were using AI to match people on the phone in call centers. For example, when you call your electricity company, instead of a random match in the call center they would use data on the agent and data (third party info) on you (the client) and decide who was best matched over the phone. They had found that revenue was directly correlated to which agent was paired to which client—analysis showed that a better match meant more revenue for the company.

So the people seemed great (CHECK).

The company was in a good position and in an emerging market (CHECK).

It was a start-up, so assuming it did well there would be career progression for me (CHECK).

James seemed like a good manager and someone that I could work with and trust. He felt to me like a leader who was a multiplier; that is, someone who uses their intelligence to amplify the smarts and capabilities of people around them. He was really curious about my experience and what I could bring to the team. After our breakfast, James asked point-blank if I would be interested in joining the start-up. Not missing a beat, I said I would definitely be interested if the package and role made sense. James confirmed he would follow up in the next couple of days to discuss the package and offering.

A week after our meeting, James called and made me an offer that was above my current salary, not by a huge amount, but enough to make it very interesting (CHECK). He also informed me that the company would sponsor my visa (CHECK-CHECK). Being duly diligent, like we've discussed in previous chapters, I asked for a training day to go into their office, get a feel for the culture, and make sure the environment and people suited me; plus I wanted to understand the technology a bit more. He agreed to a training day in a few weeks.

On my training day, I found that people in the office were super friendly and young, about my age (late twenties and early thirties). I felt a good buzz in the office. There were lots of busy people running around and I thought to myself, *I could definitely work here.*

I came to learn that there was only one other salesperson working in the United Kingdom. Unfortunately, he'd not had much luck at closing deals. Hence why James was looking for a salesperson to come in and really smash the target. Now being in software sales for the last eight years, constantly overachieving my annual target and closing big deals, my ego felt that I was more than capable to close a few AI deals. My experience ranged from closing software deals in small corporations (funeral homes—yes, they use tech) and large enterprise corporations, where they sign $5 million+ deals. So closing a deal in an AI company that was in an emerging market was going to be a piece of cake . . . or so I thought.

Using some of the negotiation tactics coverer previously, I worked with James to secure a great salary and bonus in my offer. I took the AI sales job and renewed my visa in the United Kingdom.

Starting on my first day, I was excited and the company seemed great. We had a team meeting where all thirty people who worked in the UK office gathered in the conference room and James introduced me as the "Sales Machine." I was ecstatic! For me, I had a feeling like, *This is it . . . this is where I am going to make my millions.*

During the team meeting, my manager asked me to walk them through my sales strategy and plans on how to close opportunities for the company using my previous experience. It was the first time that people were looking to me in my career for sales advice. Over the coming weeks, I spent hours putting together packages of the best sales practices from my previous experience, trainings, and classes. After learning more about the AI company, I made sales terminologies that I thought would suit the company and help us progress sales. For example, I posted the BANT slogan around the office, which I thought could be the standard process for us qualifying deals. Standard BANT terminology stands for Budget,

Authority, Need, and Time. Assuming we had all the information, each word comes with questions like, "What is the budget? Who has the authority to sign off on the deal?" etc. If people could not answer the questions, then the deal would not yet be fully qualified. The goal is to understand if the deal is real or not and decide where best to spend our resources and time. I was determined to be the salesperson that would break through the barriers and close the first large enterprise opportunity for the company in three years.

Asking some of my colleagues for help and guidance in the office, I spent time learning the technology, my sales pitch, and their story. I was constantly networking and speaking to many people across the globe. At a cricket match with a few prospective customers, I even got to meet the CEO and other executives, which made me feel like I was really part of the team.

Something started to dawn on me in my first few weeks—this company was no ordinary start-up. The people who I met and worked with at my new company were not ordinary people like I was. I come from a middle class background where we believe hard work and dedication pays off. These people came from a completely different background than me. They were on a different wealth playing field than the majority of the world's population. They were the 1 percent of the 1 percent.

Let me explain more without being able to name these people. The chief commercial officer (CCO) was in his early thirties and grew up with the British royal family. He was friends with Prince Harry. He had no experience from what I could tell in managing people or running a company, but was well regarded and promoted to CCO due to his connections and ability to leverage his relationships.

The salesperson who had so far been unsuccessful in closing a large enterprise deal was the great-grandson of Winston Churchill. Our operations director/marketing person (was never quite sure of her role) was a cousin of the royal family. The head of the French division was the son of a famous French entrepreneur, who was the CEO of one of the most powerful corporations in the country and known for his leadership.

Hopefully that paints enough of a picture for you. These were not the "normal" people I'd worked with in the past. I had never before been surrounded with this type of aristocracy, simply because where would I have met them? To top it off, the funny part was we were all around the same age, ranging from our late twenties to early thirties.

At first, I was in awe being surrounded by and working with some of the world's richest and best connected young people. Not, by any means, by what they were doing for the company, but just by their family names. These were names I'd read about in history books growing up; their distant relatives were the leaders of nations during monumental periods of world history. Each one of them was "google-able" and connected to elite global society. It was exciting to be a part of this world, even if it was just by association or the occasional "hi" at the office. I was in a new circle not available to me before.

Unfortunately for me, it was in this group of people that I realized the importance of the tiered class system in England. The foundation of British culture is a tiered class system or social class, where your family name and heritage are very important, ultimately deciding your social status and political influence. Before the 1950s, there were two different social classes, the House of Lords representing the aristocracy or hereditary upper class, and the House of Commons representing everyone else. The British monarch has always been viewed as being the top of this social structure.

Today, other factors like wealth, education, and occupation help to define your social status in England. However, at this company I started to get the feeling that there was an unspoken divide between the aristocrats and the rest of us. Even though I worked at the same company as these people, got paid more than most of them, and had gone to a good university, I had this feeling that I would always stay on the outside of this literally royal circle. Most of the aristocratic people would go for drinks together after work or hang out on the weekends at their country homes. I desperately was hoping for an invite, even though I was classed as a "no buddy American," meaning I had no famous family members, family heritage, or wealth. I really thought if I proved myself to this royal circle, they would welcome me with open arms.

My mother and father did not run any country, nor did we have any family money or heritage that was significant to speak about. We were solid American middle class, which suited us, and I was proud to be part of a society where class did not define me or my family. We value hard work and dedication, but the idea of becoming friends with my aristocratic work colleagues appealed to me. It was like I was in a movie, and I pictured myself really becoming part of this English circle. Maybe I could even get an invite to one of the royal weddings?! I would just need to prove myself to these upper-class citizens that I was worthy of their time/support and that I could help make a difference at the company.

After two months of training, the company sent me out to the field and on potential sales opportunities. There was a specific deal that they were trying to close, and they asked me to take the lead on the account and close out the opportunity. I was ready to get my hands dirty and use my sales tactics I had developed over the years through hours of hard work, learning, and experience.

From what I could gather, it was now eight months into the sales cycle and from experience, I knew if there was a chance to close out the client, it was necessary to meet in person. The client was up in Northern England, and I traveled with my colleague who was good with numbers and would assist me in the negotiations.

We spent hours looking over the numbers and calculations, putting together offers and different options on how we could close out the client and come to an agreement. I personally used every strategy I had learned, from the basics to more creative methods of building a large businesses case to prove out the value. We worked the deal hard, but found issues at every angle. The customer would not agree to our price, and we could not give away the product for free. Once we got close, the goalpost would move, and it wasn't the price, but something in the contract they didn't like.

After my fifth trip up north to meet with the client, I silently vowed not to leave their office until we walked away with an agreement. We had another pass with the client's analysis guy leading the negotiations on the new improved numbers. Again, we came to a point where they said they would not move, so I asked for the room and said I would call my boss to discuss.

For two hours we worked the numbers and we came up with a deal that would give them all the benefits. I called the analysis guy back into the room and offered a take-it or leave-it deal. The offer guaranteed the client more revenue through using the AI technology and it left us barely any profit, but the thought process was to land the deal and grow it later. Selfishly I wanted my first deal to prove myself, so I was pushing hard for the close.

The client was unsure we were actually a new technology, and they were not used to a pay-as-you-go model. So the company in the north decided that our technology was not for them and basically told us "no deal" that day.

OK, so we . . . no, wait, I FAILED.

It was not the first time I had heard "no" in my career as a salesperson. This is normal. But what was most astounding was the reaction I got from my colleagues and how it changed my position at the company. They were not surprised by our ability to not close the deal, having seen this many times before; new kinds of AI technology are not an easy sell. My confidence definitely wavered, but I was positive that we would continue and find a win elsewhere. It was almost as if, by not closing the deal, my status at the company moved down a few notches, especially with my aristocratic colleagues. I was already at a lower level since I didn't have any upper-class blood in me, and by not being able to close, especially when expectations were set high by my own management, it put a further divide between me and them. Instead of getting support from my management and pushing me to try again, I received unhappy emails and calls with their frustration that we did not close the deal.

I was now almost three months into my role. My direct boss James, who had brought me into the company, decided to take a role in the United States, thus leaving the UK office. In came a new boss who had an incredible résumé with valuable experience. She came from one of the top corporate organizations in the United Kingdom with experience in managing enterprise teams. Now remember, as we have discussed in previous chapters, typically you do not get to choose your boss and either you get lucky or you don't.

My new boss was a woman named Nancy, who was born and raised in the United Kingdom. The technology industry and my new company were both still very male dominated, so the fact we had a woman as a boss gave me high hopes and expectations.

Over the first few weeks with Nancy, it became quite apparent that she was, to put it plainly, a micromanager. Nancy had a very particular way with how she wanted things. She was focused on the numbers and how she was portrayed to her own management. Nancy liked to call out problems that she saw, but never really gave solutions. She would tell you she didn't like it, but would not give you the feedback to make it better. Within a few weeks, Nancy gained herself a reputation in the office for being a hard-ass. A few weeks into working with Nancy, she called me into her office.

Nancy: Hi, Shirley. Can you write a brief on the summary of the current deal? Then send to me please?
Me: Of course, no problem. Is this just for your review or for the management at the headquarters as well?
Nancy: It's for my boss. Make it straightforward. I want all the options and numbers we offered. Can you also make a graph to show the profit we are currently getting by month? You do know how to make a graph, right?
Me: I do . . . yes.
Nancy: OK, great. Actually, send it to me by this afternoon. I'll review it and then send on to my boss.

Me: OK, no problem.

I then took two hours to write up a detailed brief, along with the graphs to show our profits. I had to call people internally to get the correct numbers, but I made sure it had all the details she could possibly have wanted for the current deal.

Me: Here you go, Nancy. This is the brief and the graph you asked for.

Nancy: No, no . . . this is not detailed enough. Where is the history from three years back? We need all the information. I feel like you're not getting this. This number is not correct.

Me: OK, happy to double-check the numbers, but I got this straight from the analytics team.

Nancy: Hmm . . . [She looked up at me.] Do you think you are suited here?

Me: Wow, OK . . . Sorry, what do you mean? [Having been at the company for only four months now and Nancy for less than two, I was flabbergasted by her approach.]

Nancy: I mean, you sold software licenses before, not exactly the same as selling AI. It feels like you're not quite getting "it."

Me: Sorry, I'm not following. I'm in sales, Nancy, I sell. Whether it's licenses or AI, I feel I can definitely help make a difference. What is it you feel I'm not quite getting?

Nancy: It's just different for you. I think Arthur [a colleague on a different team] should take this opportunity to work the analytics team and redo the summary brief.

Me: Nancy, I'm happy to redo it, if you feel it's not what you wanted. If you tell me what I'm missing and give me some feedback, then I can create a new brief for our meeting.

Nancy: No, just let Arthur do it and I'll work with him to make sure it's correct.

Me: [Awkward silence] OK.

Poor Arthur, I thought, but it also made me feel horrible that my own boss didn't think I was capable of building the damn brief. From my perspective, rather than helping me succeed and giving me some feedback, it felt that she wanted to bring me down. Here we were, two of only three females in the office of thirty people, and she was already belittling me.

It didn't help that Nancy was an Englishwoman who was wholly swept up in the elite family names of this company and valued only the inner circle (a.k.a. the Churchills, royals, etc.). Every day she would spend time speaking to only the "elite" people in the office. We had an open office, which was basically just one big room with a conference room that Nancy named her office. Conversations with Nancy and the Churchill in the office went something like this:

Nancy (During the #METOO scandals that were on front pages of every newspaper): I believe I know which Lord is causing such a scandal in the House of Lords.

Churchill's Great Grandson: I think I know who it is also . . . Shall we discuss privately in your office?

Building a further divide, the rest of us non-royals rolled our eyes, pretending to ignore the reality of the office segregation that continued to be built around us. Gestures like this conversation were a constant reminder of who was in and who was out; with all the secret meetings or discussions, part of me felt like I was back in high school: the cool kids (who were the English aristocrats) and the not cool kids (everyone else). Working with Nancy was the first time in my career that I had worked with a solid Diminisher Leader.

As you recall from previous chapters, a Diminisher Leader is someone who believes they are the smartest person in the room and brings down the entire IQ of the people/team around him/her. They do not allow for creativity and suppress the ideas of the people who work with them.

A good manager puts trust in his/her employees and helps build them up instead of taking them apart and breaking them down. A good leader wants everyone's input to make tough decisions and work off of the ideas and creativity of the entire group to raise the IQ of the entire room. With a leader like Nancy, it's the opposite—no ideas are going around the room; only directions from one person.

> **Nancy to the entire team:** Here is the direction I want to take the business and UK office. Starting immediately, everyone needs to go through me before any decisions are made on behalf of our customers in the United Kingdom.

There was never any input from the team or any discussion. It was only direction and "I know best." And, of course, the threat is always there, too, of "my way or the highway." You don't like it, you can leave. And that's hard to do if you've just changed jobs and your visa is linked to this job.

Me: Nancy, I'm thinking of reaching out to a few telecommunication providers to see if they would be interested in our solution. I have a few contacts from my previous company that we could use. What do you think?

Nancy: We've already tried that . . . Focus on the one account you have now as that's the most important. I'm not sure why James put you on the account as you really aren't suited for it. It's a big job, and I just don't think you are going to be able to do it.

Me: Nancy, I've managed a lot of accounts in the past. Is there something you don't think I'm doing correctly? Anything you want me to change?

Nancy: No, it's just you. I don't think you are the right fit.

More importantly for me, it felt like my direct boss did not like me, which was a huge problem. Your boss keeps you employed, puts you up for promotions, and is a huge sponsor for or against you in the company. Nancy seemed to not only dislike me, but also took large measures to make me feel uncomfortable in the workplace by putting me down constantly in my abilities as a professional.

So . . . within six months I FAILED for the second time.

People don't leave bad jobs, they leave bad bosses.

Now I've hadn't been able to close a deal, and I had a boss that I did not sign up with who disliked me and only valued the people in the royal circle of the company.

Surprisingly, I had not had a lot of contact with my CCO except for a call during my interview. This was a tad concerning as he was the head of sales at the company and there were only ten salespeople across the world. At this company, there was no formal sales process or training on the technology, and six months in, I had one official account which I was running that was an established flagship for the company. The account was top-of-the-mind for all, especially for our COO, as he had closed the original deal with this company and unfortunately we only had three live accounts in the United Kingdom.

My colleague called me one morning in a panic and informed me that the one flagship account we were looking after was not aware of the new deal/renewal agreement we had reached with upper management. They wanted to "turn us off." Confusingly, we'd heard directly from our CCO just two days prior that he had spoken to the execs on the customer side and they'd agreed to the renewal. The executives had requested that they work within their organization to relay the message. Unfortunately for me and my colleague, we were dealing with people at a lower level who were not yet up-to-speed and demanded that we turn off our technology immediately. For this particular customer, we had increased revenue sales by $5 million over the last three years, but the customer wanted to turn us off in their call centers as they thought we, the AI company, were too expensive.

I was literally sitting in the dentist chair when I got an email from the customer, which basically said turn us off NOW, in effect canceling our contract. My colleague, who worked with me on the account, called me immediately and said, "We need to go back to them and tell them that we reached a deal at the C-Level and we will not be turning off." I remember feeling a sense of discomfort as it's never OK to inform someone of something that should have been told to them by their own team/management. No one likes to be in the dark.

But I reluctantly agreed with my colleague as he was adamant that if they turn off/cancel our contract then we would be in big trouble. We needed to stay "ON" in order to keep our own revenue intact. We sent the following email to the customer:

Dear Lisa and Team,

Hope you are well.
From my understanding, your CTO and my CCO spoke a few days ago and it seems we have agreed a way forward. As a precautionary can you please acknowledge your company is aware of this agreement and there is no action on your side to turn us off?

Best,
Shirley

Putting away my phone I continued with my dentist appointment as I was getting a cavity filled. Reflecting on the event as I sat in the chair, I felt a level of discomfort, but we needed to do what was right for our company and make a call, which I did. As I left the dentist office I looked down at my phone and saw WhatsApp text messages from my CCO, which were the following:

CCO: What the **** did you do?? ARE you an idiot!?! Why did you tell the customer we would NOT turning off????

CCO: That information was supposed to come from their own team NOT FROM US!

I was flabbergasted that my CCO was swearing and cursing me out via WhatsApp. Keep in mind that I was still only a few months in (six months) and that was the most interaction that I'd had with my CCO ever, and his first text message to me had the F word in it . . . Fantastic!

Me: Can we speak please? Let's discuss.

CCO: No I cannot and you've just undermined the client. They called me in a panic and are very upset as our conversation was supposed to be private and not shared with the greater team internally yet.

Me: Let me send you the email I sent. [I put it into the conversation.]

CCO: It was up to the executive to speak with the decision makers, not for you to tell them! I will have to find a way to recover this, which is not good. Myself and the executive were on the same page and in no way did we agree a way forward.

CCO: Btw—this email is not good in a few ways . . . will send some time with you at some point to explain why . . . in the meantime please read *How to Win Friends and Influence People* by Dale Carnegie.

Me: OK, please read the email chain I sent you as explains how this all came about.

CCO: I don't have time to read emails!!! [message shortly deleted from WhatsApp]

CCO: Please speak to someone else!!!! I have run out of time

Being in the workforce for almost nine years, I'd never had anyone EVER speak or act this way to me in a professional and even personal setting. I was shocked, especially because this guy is supposed to be best friends with Prince Harry. Every movie I've seen portraying the royal family makes them seem to be super polite and well-mannered. Obviously, this guy was not part of the royal family, but I'd assumed he would be of the same caliber. How wrong I was.

To be honest, I went home and had a good cry. I was already feeling unsettled in my job with the new boss, Nancy, who continued to undermine me and now, getting cussed out by the CCO was just the icing on the cake for me. You want your upper management to like you and be a supporter for your career at the company. This experience really made me sit back and reflect on where I was working and the values that I desire in my own working environment. My confidence was sinking, deals were not closing, my bosses didn't seem to appreciate me or like me, my skill sets was underutilized, and I felt isolated. From his text messages, my CCO was obviously not fond of me. And to be quite honest I wasn't fond of his rude demeanor toward me, either.

Yet again . . . I FAILED. Yes, I was between a rock and a hard place, following a recommendation from a coworker. But it still felt like a failure.

What do you do when you fail? Do you throw up your arms and get out? Or do you keep fighting? For me personally, I decided to power through at that moment. Giving up was not something I was ready to do just yet. My thoughts were: *keep going and it'll get better. It has to.*

At month seven, we had come up to our official renewal with paperwork for the big customer. They were now ready to finalize the renegotiations. My CCO had recommended that I lead the negotiations with the help of my new boss, Nancy. Nancy asked us to put together a packet on the background and history of the account. We put together a sixteen-page document that went into detail on the num-. bers, data, and relationship history since commencing the business relationship five years previously. We spent days putting this information together and double-checking to make sure it was correct with others people at the firm. We showed our new boss the draft, and she insisted that we needed more information in certain categories. So, we went back to the drawing board. We continued to make changes until she felt it was adequate and it ended up being thirty pages.

We were getting this document together for a conference call with the entire account team at our company. We would walk through the information on the call and see if anyone had any questions and then we would finalize the strategy for the customer with the renewal. This was our oldest standing customer in the United Kingdom and our most important, so we wanted to include as many details as possible.

The call was planned for 4:30 p.m. UK time in a week. I sent the packet out with all the information five days before to everyone planned to be on the call, so everyone could be prepared. We were planning to have twenty internal people join from across the globe: India, Pakistan, the United States, and Canada.

At 4 p.m. on the day of the call, Nancy informed me that she would be leading the session and walking everyone through the information. I had little choice in the matter but to say, "OK." Another blow to my ego and confidence. At 4:30 p.m., we dialed in to the call and heard twenty different clicks of people joining. The CCO joins the call and Nancy starts off the call saying something like:

> **Nancy:** Hi everyone, thanks for joining. We sent you and everyone else on the call a packet with the information we would like to discuss. Assuming you have had a chance to read through it?
> **CCO:** Actually, no, I haven't. Can you give me five minutes and I will read through?
> **Nancy:** Umm . . . OK.
> **Everyone else:** SILENCE
> **CCO:** I'm going on mute to read. Everyone stay on the line.

I had literally never seen this in my life, but the CCO kept twenty people around the globe on the conference call in silence as he went on mute and read through the thirty pages, which took close to twenty-five minutes. The rest of the people in the United Kingdom, including me, were in a conference room all looking at each other like, "What the heck?" It was such a waste of time for all of us, especially the ones dialing in from India as it was around 10 p.m. their time.

This action by the CCO was one of the most unprofessional things I've ever experienced in the workplace. It's horrible work etiquette and completely inconsiderate of people's time. From this encounter, it left a feeling in all of us that our CCO was not valuing our contribution, treating us with little consideration, and acting however best suited him. It was at that exact moment as we sat there in silence that I realized my career needed a change and I could no longer work with this posh aristocratic company, regardless of their titles or associations within the English class system. This was not the place I could embrace, and I needed to start to look for a new job immediately that had values that reflected my own.

I failed in two ways. The first was not recognizing sooner that this place was wrong and I needed to leave. I was, at that point, an experienced salesperson who'd worked in a number of companies and had closed a number of deals. As soon they replaced James with Nancy, as soon as I realized that people were getting jobs because they were someone's great-grandson, as soon as I realized that the company had an in-out group dynamic and I would always be on the out, and as soon as my CCO swore at me over WhatsApp, I should have packed my bags and left. I stayed for a stupidly long time and I have only myself to blame. Sometimes muscling through a problem is the wrong answer. Sometimes resilience is not resilience but a refusal to see what's smack-dab in front of your face.

The second way I failed is that I didn't do the job. Bottom line, in the real world, no matter whose fault it was, Nancy's or the CCO's or the English class system, I didn't close the deals.

Failure is part of the journey in your career. Every professional will go through a period of failure. It's the people who embrace it that get through it quicker. By failing, other doors open, which hopefully lead you to a better place. This experience really changed my perspective on the types of companies and people I would want to work with in the future. My focus changed to finding people and a company with my similar values, which were and remain equality for all, trust, customer success, and hard work.

None of us can predict our careers. We can have a vision and direction of travel, but the reality is your career will go up, down, sideways, backward, and full speed ahead. Be ready for setbacks and unexpected drops. Be ready for the highs that make you feel indispensable and at the top of your game. But equally, be ready to find yourself in an uncomfortable situation where you have to ask yourself, baffled and hurt, *How did I get here? How did this happen?* You may find there are times where you need to be resilient and keep pushing to achieve your ultimate goal. Again, it may not be the linear line that you project, but you'll get there in the end with the right attitude and perseverance.

Expected career path

Reality

For some of us, being resilient means that we stay in an environment that is detrimental to their health and wellbeing. You need to decide when enough is enough for you. When is the right time to make a change in your career and call it quits? Making mistakes in your career is unavoidable; it's how we handle ourselves at our lowest points that determines our success.

By the time that I finally threw in the towel at the AI company, I had given it my all, but yet continued to fail, not once but three consecutive times. Maybe it would have been different if . . . my management had supported me? Or if . . . we had a standard sales process? Or if . . . the product was more mature? Or there wasn't a divide in the company of posh upper class versus the rest of us . . . ?

So many ifs . . .

I had to forget the ifs, pick myself up, and go out to find a new job. Have you ever had to find a new job when you have low self-esteem and confidence? Let me tell you, it's not for the fainthearted. After eight months at the AI company, I had gone from being one of the top salespeople at my previous company, known for being a consistent and big hitter in a Fortune 500 company, to feeling unsure about my self-worth as a professional and questioning my own capabilities. *Maybe I wasn't as good as I once was. Maybe I got lucky before in the previous five years . . . and my luck ran out. Or maybe I was never really good and I'll never be good again.* These were the type of thoughts and questions that ran through my head.

As I was questioning my self-worth as a professional, I also had to go out and sell my abilities so someone else could hire me. Really I had two choices: stay where I was and be miserable with England's richest upper class or put on my big-girl pants and make a change happen. Knowing that my career is in my hands alone, I forced myself to get out there.

So I did exactly what we went over in the first couple chapters. Starting from scratch, I reached out to my network to grab coffee, lunch, or even an early drink with ex-colleagues, friends, and friends-of-friends. I worked on my story of why I wanted to leave the AI company: "the technology was not as mature as I was initially informed" and "In twelve to eighteen months, it would be a great time to join the company, but it's not where it needs to be now." I built my story to want to leave on the AI start-up not matching my expectations, which was, in a way, true.

The part of the story I didn't tell is how my CCO made me cry, that we were not aligned on values, our clients were unsure of the AI technology, and that there was no support from the upper management. It's not about your reality when you tell your story of "why" you want out of your current situation. Remember, no one has any idea what you are going through unless you tell them. To all my ex-colleagues and friends of friends, I was looking for a move due to the immaturity of the technology at the AI company. I told my close friends that the "rich and the famous" in England aren't all that they seem and we were lucky to not have grown up in that circle.

After reflection, this experience was a really valuable one for me. Knowing that my company and colleagues have the same values is really important to me. This experience at the AI company shaped me into becoming a better professional by knowing my boundaries of what I am and am not willing to put up with at work. I thought I knew before. But there's the theory and then there's the reality. I learned hard lessons about myself and about life, which I wasn't expecting and wasn't prepared for. I did a lot of self-examining and hard questioning. And then, even though it was incredibly hard to do, I acted on what I'd learned. I'm proud of myself for that. And when it happens to you—which it likely will, I'm sorry to say—be proud of yourself, too.

Sometimes you need to: FAIL HARDER.

ACTIVITY ON REFLECTION

1. Can you think of an example where you failed, but then continued on to do something better? Or different that you would not have experienced unless you failed?
2. Write down how you can start to be resilient and fail, but continue to grow. Maybe outside of your professional world, is there something you want to accomplish? Maybe a language or fitness goals? Do you have goals that you can plan and practice being resilient?
3. If you fail at your first go at getting a job, what's your backup plan? What is your Plan B? What will you do if you get turned down? Do you give up or keep pursuing your dreams at a different angle? Try meeting with different people?

CHAPTER 11

RESURRECTION

#MY RESURRECTION

Time to change: When you think you want to go one way, but you go another . . .

After my poor experience with the AI company and the English royals, I decided I wanted to go back to working for one of the large corporations. Due to my good record at Oracle, I knew it would not be problem to go back to them and ask for a job, but I wanted to move ahead in my career and going back felt like a step backward instead of forward.

The key was getting out of the AI company and fast, as my self-confidence was taking a plunge in that toxic environment. As I mentioned, through this experience I realized I needed to find a company with values that reflected my own like, "hard work pays off when do you the right things" and "treat others the way you want to be treated." Remembering my own advice, I decided to not quit the AI company until I found a new job, as I knew finding a new job can take potentially up to nine months. It was tough as each day stepping into that office made me uncomfortable and depressed.

Instead of putting my heart into my job like I normally would, I gave the AI job enough energy to get by and put all of my focus into getting a new job elsewhere. I would meet with people from my network for coffee, lunch, and/ or dinners to talk about their companies and careers, constantly asking, "Who is hiring?" "Do you know of anywhere looking for good salespeople?" "What advice would you give someone like me, looking for a new job at the moment?" All the basic previous questions we used in the early chapters I reused nine years into my career.

Luckily, after many lunches and coffees, I met two people—the first was an old ex-colleague, Tom, and the second, a friend of a friend, Danny. Both of them worked at a company called Salesforce, where they were currently employed. They said it was a great place to work. Salesforce is a large technology company and the leader in Customer Relationship Management (CRM) systems, now focusing on being client centric. You may have seen the logo around as it's been the leader in CRM for two decades.

Tom recommended that I apply for a job on his team. He said he would refer me in the system; plus, he'd also speak to his boss about me. As we discussed before, finding yourself a sponsor within your desired company yields a higher chance of an interview than sending in your résumé cold with no referral, and without anyone championing you into the business.

In parallel, Danny also recommended that I apply for a job with Salesforce, but on his team in the financial sector. He had been very successful in the past and said I would get on great with the team. Danny also said he would speak to his management about me.

True to their word, both Tom and Danny spoke to their management about me and the next week I was contacted by two different recruiters to discuss my previous work experience. Keep in mind that if I got hired by Salesforce, they (Salesforce) would give a referral bonus of $1,000 to either Tom or Danny if I got hired. So it's good practice to ask your company of choice if they have a hiring scheme and then find someone to sponsor you. Many companies have referral bonuses to help bring in great people to the business.

Internal recruiters are like the first-pass screeners; they make sure you are adequate and meet the job requirements that the hiring manager is interested in finding. There is a lot you can get out of the recruiter, like what is the range of salary and type of position you are applying for? Does it meet the requirements of what you are looking for in your next career move? As much as the recruiter is screening you for the position, you should be screening them on the company/role, while also trying to understand what the hiring process is.

- How long does it take to get hired at Company X?
- Assuming you put me forward, what would be the next step?
- Who is the ultimate decision maker for me joining the company? Is there a panel of people that decide if I get the job or not?
- Do you think I would be a good candidate for the position?

- Are there many people applying for the role? How many people you are putting forward to the hiring manager? If so, where would you rank me against my competition?

Get as much as you can out of the recruiter; be BOLD. During my call with the Salesforce recruiter, I learned that it was a very competitive hiring process, and that there were several other candidates they were putting forward to the business. Assuming I moved forward, the process would be to meet with a hiring manager first. Then, if the hiring manager liked me, he/she would put me forward to a panel of managers where I would need to do a presentation on why they should hire me, as well as explaining my past experience and why I am the best candidate for the role. He would send me a format/template for the session with which I could then create my own presentation. The managers on the panel would vote and decide if I would be brought into the business; they'd make the ultimate decision collectively.

At the end of the call, I asked the Salesforce recruiter if he thought I would be a good candidate for the roles. He not only thought I would be good for the roles, but agreed to put me forward to meet with the hiring managers.

I was back in the game! There was a chance to get out of this AI company and join a great firm with a strong brand in the industry. Plus, I had not one, but TWO interviews lined up at the same company to meet with different teams. Hopefully I could choose between them. I felt a sigh of relief that I had made it through the first hurdle, but it was far from over.

It was time to prep and get my general questions out to tweak them to more of a Salesforce lingo. I spent the next few days editing my answers for my in-person interviews with the hiring managers and practicing out-loud to make sure I had my story down. Why did I want to leave the AI company? Why was I interested in Salesforce?

So, I wrote out my answers, practiced out loud, and was ready for my first interview with the hiring manager on Tom's team. Walking up to the Salesforce Tower, literally one of the tallest towers in the London sky, I felt nervous, but knew I was prepared and also excited. Again, this AI company had really brought my confidence down, so it took a lot to get myself in a positive state of mind. One thing I did was look at myself in the mirror and say over and over again, "You got this."

The Salesforce hiring manager was named George. He was a lovely Englishman who instantly put me at ease as he greeted me in the lobby. The Salesforce lobby itself was impressive as there was a huge aquarium where a scuba diver was cleaning out the tank that took up the entire room. Fish were swimming above his head and believe I even saw an eel. It was extraordinary to say the least.

George and I got on great. I told him about my experience, and he sold me on the culture and environment of the company. He walked me around the office and I saw that it was a young, vibrant place to work. In the office, there were lots of people talking to one another in the kitchen with coffee and drawers full of food.

WOW. It seemed to have this start-up feel but managed to be a huge organization at the same time. We discussed the position and my background. Keeping in mind my preparation, I told him about myself and why I was interested in working at Salesforce. He listened and asked questions as to why I wanted to leave my current situation and what my goals were for the future, all questions and answers I had prepped for. From doing my research on George, I knew he was a Bristol guy and I happened to have traveled to Bristol recently, so we discussed the city and great pubs.

It was all around a fantastic conversation, which is key as it didn't quite feel like an interview since I had just as many questions for him as he had for me. Remember: prepare those ten questions and write them down! It works! At the end of the interview I asked him point-blank, "George, Salesforce seems like a great place to work. From speaking with me, do you think I would be a good fit for the role?"

His reply? "Definitely. I will put you forward to the panel."

I heaved another sigh of relief. ALMOST out of this nightmare. Dreams of leaving the AI company were now a constant part of my day and sometimes at night, too. It had gotten to the point where I tried to go into the office as little as possible. My interaction with Nancy had decreased to the bare minimum to once a week one-on-ones. I was balancing the two jobs—the job I got paid for by the AI company and my second, the job of finding a new job.

Looking for a job while you have a job is exhausting. You are doing double time. The biggest piece of advice I have for people going through this is: Put your head down and just make it happen. You are the only person who can change your situation, and whining about it may feel good, but it won't get you far.

The recruiter asked me to come back in two weeks' time for my panel, where I would present to George and five other managers on why they should hire me, as well as walk them through one of my sales cycles on a particular customer. It seemed like quite a thorough interview process since my past interviews were pretty basic. This was a whole new level of preparation that I would need to go through.

Part of me did not feel up to the task and felt just exhausted. I was tired of constantly talking to people for the past two months and doing extra work looking for a new job.

A few days after my meeting with George, I met with Danny's Salesforce manager, Jerry, another a lovely English guy. Since I had just been through this process with George, the meeting was a piece of cake. Jerry and I met for a coffee and discussed the company and the role. He was in a specific niche of Salesforce. At the end of the meeting he asked me to come back and present on a panel to him and a few other managers as well.

All of a sudden, I had two real opportunities at a great company.

Because I was going for two different roles, I had two different recruiters at Salesforce helping me. One recruiter with Danny's team was only a week into the company and was still learning his role. He was now expected to prep me for my panel with Jerry, which was in a week's time. This was unfortunate as an experienced recruiter can really help your chances and a not-so-experienced recruiter can do the opposite.

I spent the next week preparing my slides with this relatively inexperienced recruiter. It was my first real interview in over a year and I felt a bit rusty. The day before the presentation to Jerry, I walked the recruiter through my thought process for the interview: explaining my background, walking him through a deal I closed in the past without disclosing the customer, and why Salesforce should hire me.

Walking back into Salesforce for my third visit, I was excited for my panel interview. As I got into the room, I saw the three other male interviewers I'd studied beforehand on LinkedIn (the recruiter had sent me the list of people who would be interviewing me). We started with the casualties of an interview like "How are you?" and "Thanks for coming in."

Jerry eventually jumped right into it.

Jerry: Shirley, thanks for preparing for the panel, let's kick off.
Me: Great!

So, I stood up and introduced myself to the team. I started off with a review of the agenda and then paused to make sure everyone was satisfied with the agenda.

Me: Is there anything else you would like to add or change to the agenda?
Jerry: No, looks great. Thanks.

Some advice for panel interviews is to check-in throughout your interview/presentation and make sure you're on track. Most people skip this because they are so excited to throw themselves into the presentation. They forget to take a breath and have a conversation with the people in the audience. Again, you want to make this a discussion, not just a presentation.

We then went into the "Who is Shirley?" section where I explained my background and the type of person I am outside of work, which makes the discussion more personal. Everyone laughed at the photo of me and my family back in my childhood. It felt like I was off to the right start. Just as I was about to get into my customer example, the door burst open and in walked a woman with short hair and in a full pantsuit. I distinctly remember she had a rolling backpack, which she wheeled right in and sat down, apologizing for her tardiness and introducing herself to me as Zina.

I smiled and said, "Welcome."

Unfortunately for me, getting back into the interview was difficult as I was thrown off a bit by the interruption. Firstly, I didn't quite understand this woman's role and why she was in my interview. All the other people were managers and I had studied them/their roles beforehand, but this person was unknown to me. This happens in interviews and you have to be able to prove you can roll with the punches—or the interruptions in this situation.

I then started back on my customer example where I was discussing a large deal that I'd closed at my previous company. It was a retail customer up in the north of England. Having decided before with the recruiter that I was not obligated to share the customer name, I left their name out of my slides but talked about their vision and values. I described the deal cycle and interaction with their executives. Before I could get into my process and how I went about securing the opportunity for my previous company, Zina cut in.

Zina: Who is the customer exactly?

Me: I was told by the recruiter that I was not obligated to share the name of my previous customer due to confidentiality.

Zina: Why can't you tell us who the customer is? What's the problem?

Me: Again, apologies but maybe I misunderstood the brief. It was my understanding that I needed to walk you through a customer example, but did not have to disclose the customer as stated on the brief documents.

Zina (standing and pointing at my slides): Well, how do I know you aren't just making this up?

Me (shaken up and a little flabbergasted to be told I was lying. I think everyone in the room felt a little uncomfortable.): I can assure you I did not make this up, as it was one of the largest deals to close at my previous company last year.

Zina: Well then, tell us the name.

Me: Sorry, no, I won't as I told you that was not part of the brief and what I had prepared.

I now started to look around the room for some help and assistance. Jerry interrupted and came to my rescue.

Jerry: Shirley, let's continue.

Now, maybe some people could have recovered or just told her the name of the customer. But I stuck to my values that it was not appropriate to disclose the previous customer. I was completely scrambling now to prove to Zina that my deal was not made up and that it was legitimate. We continued as I walked them through the entire deal and even brought it back to how I would sell to this customer at Salesforce.

Zina continued to bombard me with questions throughout the process. "Have you ever sold cloud before?" "Why should we hire you?" "What makes you think you would fit in here?" We made it to the final slides, which frankly felt like a lifetime as I was now sweating. Remembering my own advice, I point-blank asked the entire room, "How did I do?" while knowing in the pit of my stomach the reality.

The entire room paused. Jerry responded first and said, "Let's discuss it, Shirley, and we will come back to you.

Let me walk you out." As Jerry and I left the room, he said, "Well, that was difficult. How do you feel about it?"

"Yes, it was tough. It's always good to get pushback and hopefully you got a better understanding of what I could bring to the company." I was trying to sound positive and optimistic when my heart felt heavy.

> **Me:** Jerry, what's is Zina's role as I didn't see her name on my brief?
> **Jerry:** She is the main lead at Salesforce and you would be working alongside her to help sell cloud at the perspective customer.
> **Me:** Got it.

My heart sank even further. Jerry left me at the elevators and I made my way down to the lobby and out of the building. Negativity creeped into my mind and I felt like I had definitely just fallen hard on my face during that interview. Walking home, my gut told me that there was no way I had gotten the job. Regardless, I did my follow up emails to Jerry and the rest of the managers the next day.

> *Jerry,*
>
> *Thanks for meeting with me yesterday.*
> *It was great to meet Craig, Nick, and Zina—the Salesforce team seems strong. You got me even more excited about the team, territory, and position. Given the chance, I know I could make a difference in the patch and bring more deals to a close.*
> *I look forward to hearing from you soon.*
>
> *Kind regards,*
> *Shirley*

Being diligent and practicing my resilience, I even wrote to the "difficult person" in the room. At that point, what did I really have to lose? I had the feeling that I had blown the interview, but still officially needed to wait to hear the outcome.

> *Zina,*
>
> *Thank you for your time and consideration in interviewing me for the position on Jerry's team.*
> *After our meeting, I spoke to a few people at Salesforce and learned you're one of the top performers in the UK. As you know, to be a Key Account Leader you need a strong team to help you leverage the overall platform of Salesforce. With my experience and enthusiasm to learn I am convinced that I am perfect for this role and helping you to close more business within the Service Cloud.*
> *It was lovely meeting you and look forward to hopefully speaking again soon.*
>
> *Kind regards,*
> *Shirley*

To my surprise, Zina wrote back immediately after I sent my email.

> *Hi Shirley,*
>
> *Always good to meet new people and understand their expertise and energy to sell well.*
> *Thank you for the note and glad you've spoken to other colleagues at Salesforce. I know Jerry will*

come back to you with next steps, so will leave him
to do that OK.
    Have a great weekend and good luck.

    Best,
    Zina

Jerry called me the next day and told me that the consensus in the room was that I was not the right person for the role. Zina had informed the team and Jerry that she felt "she could not work with me." He said that they would not move forward with me for that particular position.

I'd failed.

It was tough for me to get that call from Jerry, but I knew from the interview that it had not gone well, so I wasn't surprised. Regardless, hearing the feedback that they did not want to move forward with me stung. Especially since I wanted to leave the AI company so badly and get out of my horrible situation.

In the back of my mind, I knew I still had a second chance with Salesforce as I had a second panel interview the following week for a different team. My pride was hurt from not getting the initial role, and I felt embarrassed as if I didn't want to go back into their office. But I knew I couldn't give up now—especially since I had another chance.

Picking myself up after this failure was difficult, but instead of focusing on what I did wrong, I put it out of my head and put my whole heart into the task of creating a stellar story that would spark a great conversation as I led them through my slides. Knowing what I know of the process (having been through it), I completely changed my deck for the next interview. Luckily, there was a different recruiter working with me for this role and he was well experienced. He helped guide me and pushed me to reveal the name of my customer to the audience, when appropriate. I spent the entire next week poring over my slides for the interview panel.

I met with my friend Tom a few days before the interview and he told me, "Don't give up. This is a completely different set of people for this role." The role was to be a lead on the technology team, selling all the core products of Salesforce. We then went through all the people who would be in the room. I put as much detail as possible in the slides to clearly show my understanding of the customer, and what I could bring to Salesforce if they hired me. Before the presentation, I practiced out loud to my housemates and friends. I was determined to succeed and not let my previous attempt bring me down. For days beforehand, I had people quiz me or ask me difficult questions as if it was a mock interview.

A WINNER is just a LOSER who tried AGAIN.

A week went by and it was finally my panel interview day. It was my last chance to get an opportunity to work at the number one place to work in the United Kingdom and I was absolutely going to give it my all. I put on my best professional suit, so I was looking smart and feeling good. I wrote my six positive affirmations of what I was blessed to have in my life currently and what blessings I hoped would come into my life in the future while drinking my first cup of tea. They were something like this:

Thankful Blessings Today:
- I am truly grateful for my strong network of friends and family who help prepare me for my interview today.

- I am truly grateful for being a strong professional.
- I am truly grateful for being a strong and confident public speaker.

Thankful Blessings Desired:
- I am truly grateful everyone in the Salesforce interview today likes me and wants to hire me.
- I am truly grateful for giving an amazing interview that shows that I am the best person for the role.
- I am truly grateful for working at Salesforce.

As you can see, my focus was very specific on that day, but I knew what I wanted and I was going to push hard for it. I gave my interview questions/answers one more look through and sent my presentation to the hiring manager, George, before I left my flat. I reminded myself on the commute to the Salesforce Tower that I was prepared, I knew the audience (to the best of my ability), and I knew the content I was about to present. Walking into my interview that day, I felt confident that there was nothing more I could have done to prepare myself for the next hour and a half of my life in that interview panel.

Actor Jim Carrey said in the intro to a short documentary, *I Needed Color*: "What you do in life chooses you. You can choose not to do it. You can choose to try and do something safer. Your vocation chooses you." I chose to go for a role at Salesforce. I didn't take the comfortable route of letting my career slowly die at the AI company. Instead I forced myself to try to get out of the situation into a more challenging, yet also more rewarding, environment.

Again, I found myself in a room with all males presenting to them on why they should hire me. Before I went into "why me," I introduced myself to them by giving them a little background on the type of person I am outside of work, painting a picture of my personality and experiences in the world.

What I liked about this introduction was that there were no words, just pictures, which can be so powerful. We had a little laugh in the room at my family photo, and then I showed my adventurous, daring side when I talked about running with the bulls in Pamplona while living in Spain. These images helped give my audience a more personal insight into me as an individual, not just my work ethic. Connecting with the audience on the human-level early on in the interview helped to build a relationship with the people in the audience.

We humans love to connect—to make it personal. Be vulnerable and show different parts of your unique personality and life during an interview. You never know who is in the room. But someone may also be very similar to you and connect with you at that level. We continued through the presentation where I walked them through my chosen customer for the interview. Remembering what I'd learned from my first panel interview, I did not hold back and gave as much detail as possible, so they clearly understood I knew my customer well.

The interview went well. We discussed my current role, and I explained why I was best suited for the role at Salesforce. Basically, I gave examples of my role, which was completely aligned to the position that I was interviewing for that day. This is an easy way to show your interviewers how qualified you are for the position.

Throughout our discussion there were several pushbacks. The one I remember the most was, "How will you go from selling AI technology to cloud technology? As it is a very different sales cycle."

My responses were a projection, a guesstimate. No one, not even the interviewers, could answer the unknown which wasn't proven yet or argue with my answers. Simply put, "I would not need intensive training to get aligned with SaaS selling and understand the differences as I have sold it before previously. So I don't think it will be a major change for me, but just a slight change of mindset." Remember, a hypothesis is not something you can prove in the interview. Only time will prove that one true. So stand strong with your answers and be confident in your own thought process to get to your conclusion. Talk about your career aspirations and what you hope to accomplish by working at the company. People want to know that you WANT to work at their company and WHY. What attracts you to the firm? It's like dating: you don't want to continue to date someone if that person seems uninterested in you. You both want to be interesting to each other in order to pursue a relationship. So, make sure it's a balanced working relationship and both parties are bringing something to the table, just like the interview. You're not going to take a job if you don't get something in return. And people will not hire you unless they think you can bring something to the company that they don't yet have.

I had given the interview my all. The feeling in the room was positive and the interviewers were engaged and asking questions throughout our session. I was a solider on a mission. I'd failed in my first interview, but I picked myself back up and tried AGAIN. This is life. If there is one thing I hope you take away from this book, it's the importance of resilience in your career. Every day, people around the world choose to do something and become their desired future self through grit and hard work. For example, let's take celebrities, like Meryl Streep, who was turned down many times for roles and now has the most Academy Award nominations.

Describing an audition for *King Kong*, where producer Dino De Laurentiis was in the audition room with his son, who had seen the then-unknown Meryl in a play and brought her in to try for the part, Streep said: "I walked in and his son was sitting there and he was very excited that he brought in this new actress. And the father said to his son in Italian—because I understand Italian—he said, 'Que bruta? Why do you bring me this ugly thing?' It was sobering as a young girl."[6] This could have been a pivotal moment for the actress. Where one rogue opinion could derail her dreams of becoming an actress or force Meryl to pull herself up by the bootstraps and believe in herself. Today Meryl Streep has had twenty-one Academy Award nominations.

A day later I got a call from the recruiter and he officially offered me the job at Salesforce. My heart sang, and I was so relieved and excited to leave England's most entitled behind me. I swelled with pride to know that I alone got myself through a tough time by giving it my all and preserving through tough unknown waters. There's a saying that I hear quite a lot: "You're stronger than you think." Based on my experience in life—true! You don't know how strong you are or what you are truly capable of until you've been through it.

Sometimes a tough situation will make you stronger and help prepare you for what lies ahead.

Life is tough my darling but so are you.

---

6 BBC One. "Meryl Streep's Worst Audition" The Graham Norton Show: Series 16 Episode 13 Preview. 9 Jan 2015.

Remember . . . Tough times don't last, but tough people do.

So, go out there and make it happen for yourself whether you are starting out or are in a transition.

ACTIVITY

Practice thankfulness in your life. This is an activity that has really helped me in my life and can do wonders for everyone in certain and uncertain times.

How to become an even more positive thinker is quite easy. The first thing you need to do is start to appreciate what you currently have in your life. We cannot receive more from the world if we cannot appreciate what we already have. We can start by appreciating the joys of our current life: our family, friends, health, happiness, and love. The roof over our head. The education we have; the meals we can afford and the ability to eat.

The mistake many of us make on a daily basis is wishing for more: more money, more free time, and more holidays. This stops us from attracting wonderful things into our life as the focus is on what we don't have, not on counting our current blessings. We're only wishing for more. We need to change our focus from the "poor me" to the "thankful me" for what you do have in your life.

The key to being thankful for your everyday blessings is to constantly be thinking in the present tense. By keeping your thankful blessings in the present tense, they send signals to your mind (remember how powerful your mind can be) that we are truly grateful for these blessings now. When we think about these blessings, we need to feel the thankfulness throughout our body. Picture whatever it is you are thankful for in your life and truly give thanks for what you have. What joys you have in your life!

Make a list and write down these blessings. Write them down in the present tense and start each sentence with, "I am truly grateful now that . . . " Start with three things in your life that you are truly thankful for. It's best to spend a good ten minutes writing these sentences down and then reading through them three times each and really feeling the gratitude.

Blessings That You Have NOW:

1. I am truly grateful now that I have a degree from university.
2. I am truly grateful now that I live on my own.
3. I am truly grateful now that I have an internship with a top law firm.

Reread each sentence to yourself and, when you read the sentence, feel the thankfulness through your entire body. Truly and deeply feel grateful for these blessings in your life. What joy they bring to you! And how lucky you are! After you write these blessings, make a line below them and write down your thankful blessing desires. These are desires that you want in your life, but do not currently have yet. I want you to write them as if you have them now in your life.

Thankful Blessings That You Desire (write in present tense, as if you have them now):

1. I am truly thankful now that I have a full-time job.
2. I am truly thankful now that I save over $200 each month in my bank account.
3. I am truly thankful now that I feel comfortable in my role at work.

After you write down your lists of current blessings and blessing desires, reread what you wrote. Take a minute and, at each line, reach inside and feel the thankfulness for the blessing. Now, it may be hard for you at first to feel thankful for the desire list, but by thinking and feeling as if you already have it, the mind will think you actually do. You are therefore emitting emotions to your mind and thanking the world for the blessing, which is yet to come into your life. When you are thankful for it as if you have it, the world thinks you have it and will deliver it to you. This may seem completely out there to you, wacky and other-worldly, but trust me: it works.

So many of us take life for granted and do not appreciate all the blessings, however small or large in our life. Throughout history, from the philosophers, engineers, and visionaries of the past, there has been a known understanding of the power of blessings. Albert Einstein was quoted as saying, "There are only two ways to live your life. One is though nothing is a miracle. The other is as though everything is a miracle." Einstein was alluding to the fact that we have a choice in living our life: a life full of blessings that we count and give thanks for everyday or a life that is unappreciated where everything is unmoving. What type of life will you lead?

The blessings list is a powerful tool, a hidden treasure known by few. Define and clearly write down your blessings to feel the joy of receiving and having them in your life. You start to appreciate what you currently have and what you are yet to receive. Make this a morning or a bedtime ritual every day, if possible. Feel free to repeat and/or change your thankful blessings daily as you see fit. Maybe one day you focus on your job and the next your love life. Whatever it is, remember to write it in the present tense.

One of my friends, Christina, used her list when starting a new job. She had just been relocated to Mexico, having done her graduate degree in California. She was feeling timid and uncertain in the initial days of her new role—having to speak in a second language, becoming accustomed to working in an office environment, and meeting new colleagues—all very intimidating. She found herself in meetings where she could not work up the nerve to speak up or even ask questions, not wanting to look stupid or embarrass herself. After a few weeks of this, Christina called me to ask for the best way to calm her nerves at work. My answer was, "Be thankful." Be thankful for your job, your current blessings, and what is yet to come. Explaining the blessings list, I helped her form what her list could look like every morning.

Blessings Now:
- I am truly thankful now that I have a job and income.
- I am truly thankful now that I am working and living abroad.
- I am truly thankful now that I have a great apartment in a safe neighborhood in Mexico.

Thankful Blessings You Desire:
- I am truly thankful now that I feel comfortable asking questions during my team meetings.
- I am truly thankful now that I feel confident in my role and workplace.
- I am truly thankful now that my boss says I am doing a great job.

After our conversation, she started writing down her thankful list every morning before she went to work. The list would vary and change slightly each week depending on what was going on, but after repeating and feeling the thankfulness for the now/desire blessings, she started to really believe it and receive it. Two months later, I got a call from Christina saying how her boss complimented her on the questions she was bringing to their meetings. He also stated that he was very pleased to see her so comfortable in her new role.

Truly feeling and being thankful for something before you have it attracts it into your life. In order to receive, you need to put it out there to the world through writing about your desired future self and talking about what you will become. Try not to worry about the "how" this will happen or the "when," but focus on the thankfulness you feel when you will have it. Imagine what happens when you have it: what will you feel? That's the key part of this exercise—feeling and thanking the world before you receive your blessing.

CHAPTER 12

CONCLUSION

#BALANCE MY LIFE

Remember your job and what you choose to do for a living is only a part of your life. You have the whole rest of the vision board to complete as well. In this book, the primary focus was your work life and getting you started in the right direction, but don't forget the rest of your vision, which can include but is not limited to:

- Monetary wealth
- Relationships
- Health
- Location
- Purpose

To have wealth like a Steve Jobs, CEO of Apple, is almost unimaginable, but then he had health problems and died. No amount of monetary wealth could cure his cancer. To have great relationships but lack the ability to hold a job down can lead to complications in those relationships. Maybe you ask others for money or can't pay your rent, which your housemates would not like for obvious reasons. All of these compartments in your life are important and when one is not going the right way, it can leak into other aspects of your life. To keep a level head, you need to create a . . .

Balance.

How do we obtain balance? It's different for everyone and learning your right balance is a constant process. Balance is not something you find; you need to create it. Create "me" time. For some it's taking a bath or reading a good book. Others may like to just go for a walk by themselves or chill out and listen to music. Find that time to give yourself a break and do something you love for yourself.

Hobbies are a great way to disconnect, whether you like playing golf, reading, drawing, painting, playing tennis, etc. Work is NOT everything and what is important is your happiness. You have more energy when you are happy, tend to do better work, have better relationships, and so on. Exercising is a great way to create that balance. Exercise produces endorphins, which make you feel good and happy. You can't do your best work when you don't feel good. Meditation has also proven to be powerful. For a while, I was using a meditation app called HeadSpace, which taught the basics of meditation, literally giving the step-by-step how-to. I found when I was using the app that I felt less anxious in life and had more good days than I normally do.

Sleep. As humans we literally need sleep to survive. Lack of sleep can hugely unbalance you and make you feel off. A good night's sleep should be between seven and eight hours on average. Here are some suggestions if you have trouble sleeping. Melatonin is a great natural remedy to help nod you into your sleeping state. Putting your phone away a few hours before sleep and making sure to not eat too much sugar before you sleep is important. Going to sleep at ten in the evening and waking up at six or seven in the morning to go for a run before work might seem lame, but it does make you feel amazing. Whatever you need to create our own balance, try to find it.

Eat meals that give you joy and make you feel good. For me, I struggled with finding the right food for my body. For years of my life I was poisoning myself with wheat when I had an allergy and now I'm actually gluten-free. There are so many food tests nowadays that can guide you on the type of foods that suit your body and give you that energy in life. It took several doctors to realize that I was gluten-intolerant and had basically killed my gut. I had to rebuild my gut and my food tolerance from scratch. When you don't feel good, listen to your body and go get help.

Lastly, be kind to yourself. You are learning, growing, and becoming that "it." Give yourself time and don't put time-lines on things you want to bring into your life, as it may cause disappointment. For example, let's say you tell yourself, "By the time I'm thirty I want to own a house and be financially stable." What if by thirty you don't own a house yet and you're not as financially stable as you wanted? Would this cause anxiety and disappointment? My guess is probably yes, it would cause you to feel bad and not good about your situation. This is NOT helpful and does not bring positive thoughts into your head. Everything you do or think needs to help move you toward, not away from, your goal.

As we discussed in the previous chapter, it's like energy. Positive energy attracts other positive energy. Negative energy attracts negative energy. We all learned this in middle school with positive and negative atoms in physics. The rule still applies for your own personal energy and thoughts. We want to only attract positive thoughts so MORE positive things will come into your life SOON.

Instead of using timelines of when you intend to have something in your life, focus on the ultimate goal of keeping that energy positive and in the right direction. For those of you who want it badly enough, it will come into your life soon if you focus on your vision.

Many people have even achieved their goals after decades of trying. Considering this book is about being vulnerable and putting yourself and your vision out into the world, I think it's only fair for me to end on my own vulnerability. Ten years ago, I was completely broke with no money to my name. I could never imagine at the age of thirty-two that I'd be financially stable, a home-owner, living abroad, being a consistent top performer at my company of choice, married to an incredible man, and having so many international friends around the world who bring me so much joy. None of it happened overnight, but through hard work and true vision I became my desired future-self. The more I started to work, learn, and grow, the closer I became to my ultimate goal.

My vision was always to live and work abroad. Out of college, I decided that I would only work for companies that had international offices, with the vision that someday I would get transferred to another office out of America. Even though my job was to sell the technology, I never took my eye off my personal goal of moving and working aboard. Everything I did—hitting sales targets,

KPIs, and working long hours—was to help me get closer to my ultimate goal.

I didn't know how it would happen or when . . . but I knew I would continue to try as many kitchen doors or basement doors as I had to until I found my way in. Sometimes it's grit that gets you there. Others call it luck, creativity, or pure chance. But for me it's always been the vision. I would picture myself living aboard in a foreign country, traveling, and making good money. I never doubted that I would get there. I was positive and used all the resources of this book.

I'll leave you with this, and if you take away anything from my guide, take away this: "You are in complete control of your life. You can do or not do anything you want. Your limitation is yourself."

So, get started. Grow. And become! It's time to go *From Classroom to Career* and be your desired future self.

To summarize what you've learned:

✔ Decide your future with a vision board.

✔ Network like your life depends on it (because it does).

✔ Apply for jobs by finding your champion within the company.

✔ Interview the interviewer and blow them away with your preparation.

✔ Negotiate NOW and use your "if-then" statement to get MORE.

✔ Build a strong brand by being aware.

✔ Dress for the job you don't have YET.

✔ Be aware of relationships and politics on the job.

✔ RESILIENCE wins the race, every time.

✔ Balance your job and the rest of your life through doing things you love.

ACKNOWLEDGMENTS

It's true what they say, *it takes a village* or in my case a *global village* to write a book. When I started on this journey in 2017 it's the small things that helped to get me to the next phase. My friend, Emma Fish, helped me with my initial blogs. Many thanks, Emma. The first step is the hardest and you helped me to take that step. Many thanks too to my mentor and dear friend, Jon Paul (JP), who encouraged me to post an article online, and my friend, Melony Garcia, for editing my initial piece. Meeting with my first author, Helen Whitten, I learned about writing a book proposal with the detailed process and timescales. Thank you, Helen, for that important piece of guidance.

As these small meetings and sessions helped me move closer toward my goal of publishing a book, the main figures in my life continued to be unconditionally supportive, especially my parents, Ann and Chris Morrison. Although unsure why I wanted to write a book, they were always there to listen and encourage me to keep going. Many of the lessons and learnings detailed in this book are from my dad. Even though is now retired, he is to this day the best businessperson I know. As for my mom, all the contagious positivity she has brought into my life fed this book and is now being passed onto my readers. Plus my three amazing siblings, Luke, Ben, and Molly Morrison. The first person to read a chapter of my manuscript was my brother, Luke. He was just starting his first job out of school, and I particularly wanted him to read the personal brand chapter, which he claimed *was a good lesson*. That reassured me I was headed in the right direction. My brother Ben has always been willing to help, especially around building a CV/résumé, which is his expertise. Then there's Molly, my rock and best friend. She calmed me and helped keep me sane throughout this entire journey. I wish everyone could have a sister as supportive and kind as she is. My dear husband and best friend deserves all my thanks for his patience. I know writing this book took away from our time together, and he was classy as ever in showing support. I appreciated all the little things he did, like bringing me a tea when I write and giving me a hug when I need it most. He is the best thing that's ever happened to me.

Over the last twelve years I have been very fortunate to meet so many great people in the workforce, where many of these stories in this book come from. Huge thank you to Carrie Schwab-Pomerantz for being so kind to me when I started out and being one of my role models. Thank you to my first couple of bosses who helped kickstart my career, especially Pablo Otin, Ken Avery, Phil Edwards, and Micheal O'Hora (for taking a chance on a Yank). Many thanks as well to all my Salesforce friends and colleagues who brought me into the ecosystem, Danny Kolodynski, Tom Smith, Phil Neal, George Dawson, Jerry Haywood, and Craig Murray.

There have been a few people that have gone over and above for me, people who do not know me well but decided to help and give me their time. Dan Farber, our SVP of Strategic Communications at Salesforce, took time to speak with me and coach me, and reviewed my manuscript.

Thank you, Dan, for your kindness and guidance. Alex Murray, Director, Programs & Marketing Futureforce at Salesforce, was kind enough to endorse the book and help me launch it into the world. Thanks also to the support of Annie Vincent, Director of Corporate Communications and Brent Hyder, President and Chief People Officer at Salesforce. Ignacio Gallardo, the Executive Director of Career Services at UCSB, kindly took a meeting with me and endorsed the book. I so wish I had known Ignacio and his team when I went to UCSB!

I have also had mentors along the way who played a pivotal role. Many thanks to Gary M. Pomerantz, *New York Times* bestselling author and friend. He spent many sessions walking me through the challenges of writing a book and coaching me on the next steps. He was one of the first people I called when I landed a publishing contract. Also, my thanks to Jennifer Lagaly, who helped me land my first leadership role at Salesforce and has also endorsed this book. Special thanks to my own leadership team for their support: Phil Neal, Clare Brown, and Steve Hubert.

There's been many friends who have also played a helping hand, especially the girls from my Book & Wine Birthday bash who all read, corrected, and commented on a chapter. Big thanks to all my wonderful friends: Ashley Hawker, Alyce Lynch, Christa Wilde, Emily Watkins, Gemma Brown, Hillary Buckner, Hristiana Georgieva, Megan Harrison, Nanna Bergmann, and Lindsay Inston. And also to all my friends around the world, thank you for your constant support and love: Anya Tomkiewicz, Brae Mort, Katie Gerpheide, Christina Lukeman, and Lucy Mahoney. A special thanks to Jessica Dannheisser for helping me edit and realize I needed an editor. Things are never quite as scary when you've got great friends.

Thank you to the amazing team at Clapham Publishing Services. When I stumbled upon its services, I had no idea I found the best team and now friend to work with on this project. Katie Isbester, you are an inspiration and thanks for all you've done for me. You helped me bring this book to life.

Last but not least to Skyhorse Publishing Inc., many thanks for taking a chance on me! As a first-time author, I was unsure of the process. The team at Skyhorse has been professional and helpful throughout the entire process. Steven Sussman, thank you so much for kindly connecting me to the editing team, especially Caroline Russomanno, who is amazing. She understood the book and concept from the get-go. Speaking with Caroline, and then Tad Crawford, was the reason I signed with Skyhorse. They impressed me and understood the change I am hoping to bring to society with this book and get everyone (regardless of their background) on a more even playing field. Thanks also to Tony Lyons, CEO of Skyhorse, for starting such a great company with strong values. It's been a truly wonderful journey.

It is sincerely humbling to be reflecting and writing this acknowledgment. Thanks to all again for the support and love that went into this book.

Books from Allworth Press

The Art of Digital Branding
by Ian Cocoran (6 × 9, 272 pages, paperback, $19.95)

Brand Thinking and Other Noble Pursuits
by Debbie Millman with foreword by Rob Walker (6 × 9, 336 pages, paperback, $19.95)

The Copyright Guide (Fourth Edition)
by Lee Wilson (6 × 9, 304 pages, paperback, $19.95)

Emotional Branding
by Marc Gobé (6 × 9 , 352 pages, paperback, $19.95)

Employment Law (in Plain English)
by Leonard D. DuBoff, Kenneth A. Perea, Christopher Perea, and Lauren Barnes (6 × 9, 336 pages, paperback, $24.99)

From Idea to Exit (Revised Edition)
by Jeffrey Weber (6 × 9, 272 pages, paperback, $19.95)

Fund Your Dreams Like a Creative Genius™
by Brainard Carey (6⅛ × 6⅛, 160 pages, paperback, $12.99)

Intentional Leadership
by Jane A. G. Kise (7 × 10, 224 pages, paperback, $19.95)

Legal Guide to Social Media
by Kimberly A. Houser (6 × 9, 208 pages paperback, $19.95)

Millennial Rules
by T. Scott Gross (6 × 9, 176 pages, paperback, $16.95)

The Patent Guide (Second Edition)
by Carl W. Battle and Andrea D. Small (6 × 9, 336 pages, paperback, $19.99)

Peak Business Performance under Pressure
by Bill Driscoll and Peter Joffre Nye with a foreword by Senator John McCain (6 × 9, 224 pages, paperback, $19.95)

The Pocket Small Business Owner's Guide to Building Your Business
by Kevin Devine (5¼ × 8¼, 256 pages, paperback, $14.95)

The Pocket Small Business Owner's Guide to Business Plans
by Brian Hill and Dee Power (5¼ × 8¼, 224 pages, paperback, $14.95)

The Pocket Small Business Owner's Guide to Negotiating
by Richard Weisgrau (5¼ × 8¼, 224 pages, paperback, $14.95)

The Pocket Small Business Owner's Guide to Starting Your Own Business on a Shoestring
by Carol Tice (5¼ × 8¼, 240 pages, paperback, $14.95)

Positively Outrageous Service (Third Edition)
by T. Scott Gross with Andrew Szabo and Michael Hoffman (6 × 9, 224 pages, paperback, $19.99)

Star Brands
by Carolina Rogoll with foreword by Debbie Millman (7 × 9, 256 pages, paperback, $24.99)

The Trademark Guide (Third Edition)
by Lee Wilson (6 × 9, 272 pages, paperback, $19.95)

Website Branding for Small Businesses
by Nathalie Nahai (6 × 9, 288 pages, paperback, $19.95)

To see our complete catalog or to order online, please visit *www.allworth.com.*